SNOW

MEN
a guide for guys

Text and Drawings
by
Chickie Rosenberg

author of
Snowboarding for Women: a guide for the Betty Shred wannabe

Show Dog Snowboard Press, LLC
Box 1069
Killington, Vermont 05751

www.SnowboardingforMen.com

ISBN 0-9744658-1-X
Library of Congress Control Number: 2004094809

First Edition, 2004

Question and Answer snowboard jokes are courtesy of Dave Bennett, Keith Hopkins, and Willa Scantlebury.

Printed in the United States of America

Daamen, Inc. Printing Company
Industrial Park
West Rutland, Vermont 05777

INSPIRATION

I owe my inspiration for this endeavor to the wonderful people to whom I have given snowboarding lessons. Their overwhelmingly enthusiastic response to my coaching has provided a positive endorsement of my approach to teaching.

DEDICATION

I dedicate this book to my husband Paul Rosenberg who has given me the support and encouragement to pursue my love of snowboarding. He was incredibly enthusiastic about my first book, *Snowboarding for Women: a guide for the Betty Shred wannabe,* and his insistence that I give "equal time" has led me to write this gender specific version for men. Paul is also my lawyer, my business advisor, my proof reader, my indefatigable source of creative ideas, my publicist, my best book salesperson, and my star snowboarding student.

WARNING-DISCLAIMER

This book has been written to provide information on snowboarding. It is a guide in preparing a person in terms of how to dress, necessary accessories, selection of equipment, and what to anticipate when learning to snowboard. It is not intended to be a do-it-yourself guide nor is it at all a substitute for a professionally directed lesson. In fact, it is not even meant to be a guide book for other instructors, as different snowboard professionals follow their own procedures for teaching and have their own methods of instruction.

Learning to snowboard can be a positive experience, despite the physical risks inherent in the sport. The purpose of this book is to avoid unnecessary exhaustion, discouragement and possible injury. Hopefully, by explaining what could take place in a lesson it will not only provide a guide but be an impetus to taking a lesson with a qualified instructor.

The author has tried to cover subjects of importance to the beginner snowboarder; however, the information discussed herein should be interpreted as a highly individualistic and often idiosyncratic guide and not as an ultimate source for snowboarding information. Furthermore, this book contains information on snowboarding equipment and web sites that are current only up to the printing date.

The author and publisher will not be responsible to any person or entity for any injury or damage alleged to have been caused, directly or indirectly, by any of the information or instructional procedures described in this book.

ABOUT THE AUTHOR

This is Chickie Rosenberg's second book on snowboarding. The first book, *Snowboarding for Women: a guide for the Betty Shred wannabe,* was an immediate success with book signings, speaking engagements, interviews, and articles in both local New Jersey and Vermont publications plus a write-up in *The New York Times.* More importantly, letters and e-mail from readers validated Chickie's very special approach to snowboarding instruction and specific preparedness for this snowsport.

In 1990, Chickie Rosenberg began teaching snowboarding as one of the original staff of seven instructors at Killington Ski and Snowboard Resort in Killington, VT, the largest ski and snowboard resort in eastern North America. Today, she is part of their snowboarding team of more than one hundred snowboard pros. Over the years, Chickie has taught more people who have, in turn, become snowboard instructors than anyone else on the Killington staff. She has developed a wide reputation for coaching and is known for giving a *no falls* lesson which has earned her a following of loyal students. Her achievement of the coveted Level II certification by the American Association of Snowboard Instructors (AASI), her years of teaching, active participation in regional training clinics, and extensive riding at resorts in North America, South America, and Europe have given her a broad perspective on the thrilling experience of snowboarding.

Chickie is a frequent contributor to *Snow Pro*, the official publication of the Professional Ski Instructors of America-Eastern Education Foundation (PSIA/AASI). She also wrote a series of articles for *Fresh and Tasty,* a snowboarding magazine. Chickie is the editor of *Show Dog,* Killington's in-house publication, which goes to a teaching staff of over 500 instructors.

Just in case you may think of a snowboard instructor as lacking in diverse cultural interests, Chickie is a docent at The Newark Museum in Newark, N.J., where, along with giving art tours to the public, as an expert in African art she has written on the museum's collection, *Art of Africa: The Newark Museum Knowledge Cards,* recently published by Pomegranate Communications, Inc., Catalog Number K151, Box 6099 Rohnert Park, CA 94927, www.pomegranate.com.

An undergraduate degree in English at Muhlenberg College and an M.A. from New York University are academic credentials, and years of teaching on the high school and college level plus communication skills applied in free lance writing are but one part of the picture of an energetic and enthusiastic coach. But the true essence of her talent which has made her outstanding in her field is the fact that Chickie has a deep love for snowboarding. In this book she has set out the guidelines, explained the process, offered advice on taking lessons, and written a very detailed account of everything to expect.

So, what are you waiting for? Get started reading and be ready to ride.

CONTENTS

INTRODUCTION

My first book, *Snowboarding for Women: a guide for the Betty Shred wannabe,* was so well received that it sold out the first edition in less than two months. That book's focus was an encouragement for women to enter the sport of snowboarding. Men do not tend to need such coaxing, judging by the fact that there are five and a half million snowboarders in America and three/fourths of them are men. When doing book signings for male purchasers, I found myself crossing out the Betty Shred reference and writing "for rad dudes too!" Thus, I knew that I must write this book, *Snowboarding for Men: a guide for guys.*

Here is the situation: your friends are all excited about snowsports, and you would like to join them for a get-away in the mountains. Skiing is a popular sport, but snowboarding is really where it is at nowadays. *Snowboarding for Men: a guide for guys* was written for those spirited independent men out there who are reluctant to learn snowboarding in a conventional manner. These are the ones I see bashing their bodies on the hill in an attempt to learn "on their own." You don't want to be injured, and also, you don't want to look really stupid trying to do something you know nothing about. You would quickly find out that you cannot muscle your way into learning how to balance on a snowboard. That is where this book serves a vital purpose. Although not attempting to be a substitute for a lesson, I will try to save you, the aspiring snowboarder, from the typical crash and burn method of self instruction!

My advice: take a lesson. This book will prepare you for what to expect in a professionally guided coaching situation and hopefully encourage you to join in, rather than go through the frustrating experience of trying to learn without instruction.

If you are hesitant because your friends are all advanced skiers or snowboarders who would not be with you (or even if you have no one to go with to the resort), that is rather an advantage in some ways. The group introductory lesson will offer a sense of privacy in that your friends will therefore not be witnesses to your clinic situation. One loses self consciousness when learning in a group of strangers who are all in the same situation of being newcomers to the sport. Another plus of the group lesson is that people tend to bond. Although the actual time spent together in the lesson may be brief, relationships are forged, resulting in your having met people on your own ability level with whom you can practice riding after class. An extra bonus will be the fact that because you all learned together, you will have in common a shared knowledge and mutual understanding of standard snowboarding basics.

It's a guy thing. Men do not speak of hesitation to ride a chairlift, but that does not necessarily mean that it isn't an anticipated anxiety producing experience. Don't worry about riding on the chairlift. Everyone manages to do it. I find it akin to the fact that I fly in airplanes. I don't enjoy flying, but, nevertheless, I still do so rather than face alternative modes of transportation. Ground level lifts are called "drags" in Europe, and I think that is a fitting description as these surface lift methods of propulsion are simply to drag a person uphill. The most nervous I have ever been on a lift was in Chile when taking a seemingly never ending t-bar. The rope tows, pomas and t-bars in the United States are not quite so harrowing, although in comparison, the chair lift starts to look very appealing.

Among the advantages of the chair lift is that it moves quickly, one is usually not alone so there is companionship to help relieve personal stress, and I just don't look down. Most men don't have a problem with heights or at least don't admit to it, but if vertigo is one of your hidden fears, don't worry. I have been instructing for ever so many years and have skied and snowboarded all over the world, but I never ever look down from a chairlift. The best way to defeat vertigo is not to let it happen. Anyway, by the time you'll get to taking a chairlift, you will be stoked on snowboarding, so fear of heights will not be a deterrent. Another comforting fact is that most of the larger ski areas have trams or cable cars to whisk you up the mountain. The same rule applies there as for the chair lift: look out, look up, but don't look down!

Injury is always a possibility, but if you are cautious and if you take a lesson with a professional instructor, you should be safe. Whenever I question persons about an accident, it is usually due to being on terrain which was above their skill level, or they were fooling around, or they had a friend coaching them. Knowing how to ride does not mean knowing how to teach someone to ride. Unfortunately, the most commonly stated words of encouragement one hears on the mountain is, "Don't worry. You can do it." This is said by the friend who has placed his companion in a situation having overestimated that person's ability to handle it. What is easy to do for an experienced snowboarder is far from easy for the novice. Even if the skill level is there, the scene is set for injury. Don't let this happen to you. Take a group or private lesson with a snowboarding professional.

The best counter to such a situation is development of the necessary skill level for the terrain you have selected. Practice the proper moves and take repeated lessons because a clinic from last season or even last month becomes vague in your memory, and you may be wasting the opportunity to improve by practicing what are poorly remembered or improper movements and thereby embedding those errors into your riding style.

In case you have already “tried” it, that doesn’t really mean you have mastered snowboarding. An unfortunate situation is that in marketing the sport, ski areas tend to advertise a learn to snowboard lesson with the implication that this initial clinic will be the total instruction you will ever have to take. Learning to snowboard simply means learning some of the basics. There’s a lot more to it all than could ever be taught in several hours and than could ever be absorbed in such a short time. I often wonder about people who proudly state that they have had one lesson and then gone on a black diamond (expert) trail. Do they think that having done so means they are experts? I interpret it that they are rather stupid and were lucky to have come down unscathed! And snowboarding is not simply a modified form of sledding with the fastest one straight down as the winner. Far from it. This is a sport requiring rhythm, balance, and precision of body movement, rather than flying straight until the inevitable crash landing.

What is really necessary in learning to snowboard is simply an understanding that one must persevere in learning very specific movements until mastery. Those are the necessary ingredients along with stubbornness and a determination to succeed. There are no wimps who snowboard. It is not a simple process to snowboard, so those who try to muscle their way through in a hit or miss strategy and those who like a quick learn do not last very long in the sport. On the other hand, the guy who insists that he will meet the challenge and focuses on attaining precise skills will certainly finish up as an accomplished **radical dude !**

ORIGINS

The year was 1965. Sherman Poppen was experimenting with creating a snow toy for his daughter. He bolted together two skis, put a plank on top, and *voila*--- the very first snowboard! One year later, with skid pads for foot stability and a rope at the front, it was successfully marketed to the public as the Snurfer. The rest is snowboarding history.

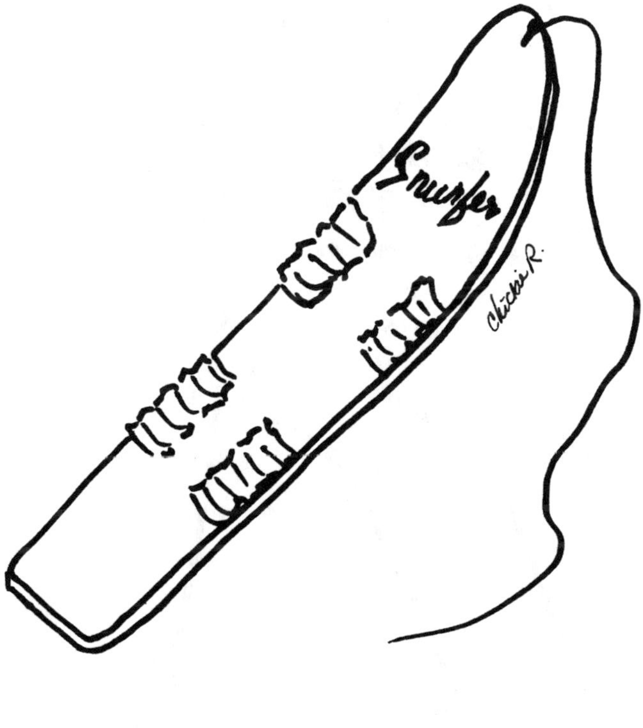

TOP FIVE
answers
1. It's called a Snowboard
2. Yes, it's FUN
3. No, it's actually quite easy
4. Yes, I can stop
5. No. I don't ski anymore
Chickie R

CHAPTER 1

ANSWERS/QUESTIONS

Around 1990, *Transworld Snowboarding* magazine sold an "answer" shirt which had the following message emblazoned on its back:

Top Five Answers

1. **It's called a snowboard.**
2. **Yes, it's fun.**
3. **No, it's actually quite easy.**
4. **Yes, I can stop it and even turn!**
5. **No, I don't ski anymore.**

If those were the answers, then what must have been the questions?

Question #1 must have been: What is it?
Answer #1: It's called a snowboard.

Back then, answer number one was not so very obvious. It was not unusual for snowboarders to be one of a very select few to appear at mountain resorts. In fact, the very rarity of meeting a fellow snowboarder contributed to an overall spirit of comradery. Age and sex were not factors, and method of snowsport transportation became a means of entry to friendship with snowboarders greeting each other and taking runs together, simply for the novelty of riding with a fellow boarder. Even today snowboarders are pleased to meet fellow riders on trails. Regarding the equipment, it constantly amazes me that people are always mistakenly calling my snowboard a *skiboard.*

Question #2 must have been: Is it fun?
Answer #2: Yes, it's fun.

Although I am obviously wearing my resort instructor's uniform, people constantly ask me if I like to snowboard. Would I be doing it if I didn't like it? My answer to the preference over skiing is that snowboarding is simply much

QUESTION:

HOW DO SNOWBOARDERS GREET YOU ON THE SLOPES?

ANSWER:

SORRY, DUDE!

Chickie R

you should know that the most common snowboard injury is to the wrist, caused by the person reaching out with arm extended to prevent falling. Instead of breaking the impact of a fall, the result is often a broken wrist! There are snowboard gloves with built in wrist protectors and some people use in-line skating wrist guards. If you are worried about a wrist injury, I advise wearing wrist guards, although I have mixed feelings on the subject. Wrist guards are awkward, making it difficult to adjust bindings or do other fine motions. A second negative is that the shock of impact is then merely transferred to the next joint, the elbow. Look at your wrist. It is absurd to expect this body joint to support the thrust of your entire body. It is simply much easier to keep hands pulled to the body, and, if feeling a loss of balance, just sit down. Never reach out to brace yourself from a fall. However, that's easy advice to say to people but not always so simple to for them to do in quick reaction time, particularly if you will be headed to the half pipe or doing tricks in the snowboard park. If those are your destinations, better get those wrist guards.

DaKine at www.dakine.com, RED at www.redprotection.com, Pro-Tec at www.pro-tec.net and Drop Gloves at www.dropmfg.com are all companies for wrist guard protection. Check them out, and it will be one less thing to worry about.

Note the bold typeset: **I absolutely encourage all of my clinic participants to wear knee pads,** thus developing an automatic reaction of dropping to the knees. In terms of injury protection, inserted pads will cushion your knees from impact but more importantly, the primary reason to wear them is because then you will never hesitate to forcefully drop to your knees the moment you are off balance, thus eliminating the reflex of reaching out with wrist extended or falling onto one's shoulder. Where do you get knee pads? Available at snowboard shops are those specifically for snowboarding or equally good are pads for telemark skiing. You can even go to Sears or Home Depot and check out the roofer's pads. You can also use rollerblade knee pads. Any of these will do, as long as they are comfortable to wear and stay in place. Don't worry about how they look as they will be on your knees, inside the pant leg.

I cannot stress enough the use of knee pads. Another bonus aspect of knee pads is because snowboarders spend a lot of time either sitting or kneeling, and when kneeling, your knees get really cold. Padded knees are definitely the single most important requisite for both body protection and general comfort, and they are particularly important to have for that first lesson. Just remember, the primary reason to have padded knees is not to offer comfort to that body joint, but rather, to prevent wrist and shoulder injury. Broken wrists or injured shoulder rotator cuffs are not a lot of fun, and it ruins a nice day of riding.

A second possible injury risk area is the tail bone. I've personally never fallen backward hurting my tail bone, but many people complain of such an injury. A very simple solution for protection would be to take a washcloth folded into a small square and positioned inside your long underwear. Burton has a product, the Burton Impact Short, which has padded protection for the tail bone and hips. There are several such snowboarding specific items now on the market. These are similar to what boys who play football refer to as a "girdle," available at neighborhood sporting goods stores. I have recommended this item, particularly when I am working with someone who is disabled and at high risk in terms of injury. There is a company in Oregon called Crashpads which will give you a full array of padding choices. Check them out at www.crash-pads.com.

I once gave a snowboard lesson to a person who enthusiastically believed in protective padding. He wore all of the standard in-line skating gear of helmet, elbow pads, knee pads, and wrist guards, plus pants which were designed with strips of padding on the upper thighs. When asked if he was afraid of injury (which certainly seemed to be an understatement), his reply was not what I'd expected. "How could I possibly get hurt with all this protection?" was his optimistic answer. He had no fear of injury and therefore was easily able to concentrate on his new learning experience. This is an extreme case, and such extensive equipment is rather cumbersome, but perhaps there is something to be said about his approach.

Several years ago I attended a snowboard camp and found myself in a reverse position in that I was among the students rather than in the role of instructor. I was absolutely astounded at the confessions of my fellow classmates in their descriptions of extensive padding to prevent injury. They wore knee pads, wrist and elbow pads, tailbone pads, and even hockey shoulder pads. You name it, they padded it! Again, if there is no fear of injury, one is less tentative, leading to a more positive performance, and the fact that snowboard clothing is so loose enables one to discreetly pad to excess.

Absolutely to be considered in the category of safety is wearing a helmet. I had already been wearing a helmet for several years when celebrity ski deaths focused a great deal of attention on the subject of helmet safety. It is not really determined whether helmets would have prevented death in the cases of Sonny Bono or Michael Kennedy, both of whom struck trees. According to an article in the Winter 1998 issue of *The Professional Skier* (published by PSIA, Professional Ski Instructors of America) entitled "Helmets Gain Popularity in Snowsports Industry" by Julie K. Hall, helmets offer protection "from impact with a stationary object at 12 miles per hour...[and] skiers involved in fatal collisions are generally skiing faster than that." If this subject makes you really nervous, however, you can put the risk factor into perspective. According to Jim Russell, M.D. of the Killington Medical Clinic, head injuries in winter sports account for 2.5% of all injuries, as opposed to 5% in soccer, 87% in professional boxing, 10% in college football, and 20% in high school football.

Nevertheless, wearing a helmet does offer protection from and reduce the severity of concussions. I once had a major crash in my early years of snowboarding (in all honesty, my only one ever of its kind, but once was enough). I was feeling overconfident and certainly going too fast when I lost my balance, leaned back (oh, no!), and must have resembled a cartoon character whose head was going *boingg boingg* as it bounced on the snow. Also I have seen skiers and snowboarders alike who crash their heads on lift chairs or are bashed in the head by ski toting resort guests. The helmet offers excellent protection from such dangers. An added bonus for me is the fact that on those days of extreme wind chill, the helmet keeps your head toasty warm.

If all this talk has frightened you, a *Wall Street Journal* article of January 12, 1998, pointed out that safety and sound judgement are the important factors in terms of mountain safety and head injuries. The article quotes Terence Davidson, professor of surgery at the University of California at San Diego and a 30 year veteran of the Mammoth Mountain Ski Patrol, who states that most impact injuries are not really skiing/snowboarding accidents, but instead occur by those persons who "happened to be on skis while doing something stupid." See the listing of helmet products in the Appendix area of Chapter 3.

I would **not** advise anyone to snowboard who has a bad back. The risk of doing damage outweighs the positive experience of having fun snowboarding. For those who like to wear fanny packs or backpacks, if you do this while snowboarding, you may wind up with a bad back, so leave those items in the locker.

The point of all this is not to frighten anyone, but it is unrealistic to assume that we are immune to injury. Snowboarding does have its risks, although I have always maintained that it is safer than skiing. Wrist bones heal, whereas the skier's knee injury of a torn ligament requires complicated surgery. Also, a most important aspect of injury prevention is personal conditioning. Although at my ski area we like to believe that within the on-snow time of our standard group lesson you can learn to snowboard, this is based on the presumption that the guest is in reasonable physical condition. Lower expectation should be made for couch potatoes who never take part in any physical activity, for those who are exhausted after the long drive from home to the ski area the previous night which resulted in less than their normal hours of sleep, and for those who were out partying with alcohol consumption causing an element of dehydration. All of these factors contribute toward the risk of injury. Be practical about this adventure, and give it your best effort by proper preparation in terms of general conditioning.

Fear

The problem with fear is not always due to its origins. Some fears are realistically conceived, others falsely; nevertheless, perception is reality. This means that if you **think** that something is dangerous or frightening, then it **is.** Logical explanation has no role here. A result of fear is often a physical one in that muscles tense up. Your fear, which has sent a message of "I know that I can't do that" or "I know that I will be hurt,"results in a stiffening of body muscles which guarantees a sort of wish fulfillment of your assertion in that you certainly will not be able to make the proper moves, thus truly creating a situation of higher risk of injury. What does one do with such a head case? Just avoid the situation where fear is in the driver's seat. Stay with a qualified instructor and build your confidence based on the reality of your skill level.

In the Introduction is a confession of my fear of heights. Women tend to voice this phobia at the very mention of setting foot on the ski/snowboard resort scene. Many men also have a dislike of heights, even though they often do not mention it. First of all, as a beginner at most resorts you usually will not be going high up on the mountain as that terrain would tend to be too steep for your ability level. Secondly, there are various ways to deal with the tendency to have vertigo. One looks straight ahead, not down, to avoid that sinking feeling. Or, don't look out at all! Your instructor will guide you in lift usage (see Chapter 10 for specifics on how to take a chairlift), and there are other options of lift systems which are either enclosed or on the ground surface.

That was always one of my biggest fears: how could I become a ski instructor if I had a fear of heights? I've kept my eyes squeezed shut many times, particularly in Europe, asking my chair partner when it was safe to open them and getting a running report of the spectacular sights I was missing. It's not really a big deal. If I could work it out, anyone can.

Machismo inhibitions prevent men from confessing fear but that doesn't mean it's not there. It's a funny thing with fear. Fear can create a certain degree of tension and anxiety which may be an asset. You are pushing yourself to achieve and conquer your fear with a result of intense exhilaration at your success. On the other hand, fear can create paralysis. Muscles and joints go rigid, and you absolutely are no longer physically capable of enacting the moves you know you should make.

The first way to deal with such fear is simply to avoid these situations. Do not join friends going to places which you know will be beyond your skill level. When your lesson ends, be sure to ask your instructor which areas on the mountain would be appropriate for you. Remember that trails tend to get "skied off" in the late afternoon which means that the snow surface will have become slick. This is due to the fact that by now softer snow has been pushed aside as a result of the accumulation of skier traffic during the course of the day. Changing light and afternoon shadows causing vision difficulty plus drops in temperature are additional factors to be considered. Fatigue is another element. I never take a "last run" but instead stop the previous run before I am too tired to really enjoy it fully.

New riders tend to become tense and fearful when on a busy trail. Basic insecurities come to the fore as one not only has to contend with the elements of riding skills, but also there is the worry that someone else will be lacking in their own skills and crash into us. For some reason, people seem to come clumped in waves of groups down a trail. The best advice is to go to the side, out of the way, and wait a moment until things quiet down, and then you can regain your concentration and composure. Remember that the sound of the snowboard can also create fearful situations for others. That is why it helps to call out "on your right" or "on your left" to the person you are overtaking. Taking control of a situation can help reduce your own fear factor as you find your way through the crowds.

Some coaches advise singing while you ride. Song helps in that it relaxes you and also induces rhythm which will remind you to even out your turns (we all have a tendency to hold onto and favor one direction of a turn longer than the other). Nervousness can actually cause you to unconsciously hold your breath. Counter this tendency by doing some deep breathing. Smiling also helps, as does self-imaging. Focus on how well you are doing, rather than worrying about what is ahead. I always tell my students to stop and look back. See how far you have come, and be impressed that it was over such challenging terrain. Instead of being your worst critic, try being your own fan club, and give yourself some pats on the back.

No matter how experienced or advanced a rider we are, there is always a place or circumstance which can unnerve us. We become frozen, unable to initiate a move! Here is where imaging and the power of positive thinking come into use. Imagine how you would *like* to ride this trail. Creating a mental picture will help lead the way. Take it in small portions in that you need not do the entire distance. Instead, just deal with a limited number of turns to go part way. Then tackle the remainder.

One reason why this situation may arise is the fact that seeing a line of skiers or boarders all stopped at the height of a trail has the power of suggesting to you that something horrendous is ahead, out of sight but just over the ridge. Resist the urge of stopping in their company, not only because their fear is contagious, but also because you would have lost your rhythm which makes it hard to begin again. Pass through the crowd, and proceed forward with due caution, but proceeding nevertheless.

The key to controlling fear is to have confidence. The way to have confidence is to build upon success, and the road to success is "mileage." Work and rework those basic skills with miles of experience on appropriately challenging terrain before adventuring to a higher level of difficulty. As to the reputation of the first snowboarding lesson as a punishing experience, I honestly believe in a "no-crash" lesson. That applies to my group clinics along with the private lessons. It really is not necessary to have first time snowboarders flying out of control and crashing; that is not a positive reinforcement method of learning. Instead, a good coach will guide the group in a sequence of maneuvers which are success oriented.

The true problem is in identifying that "good coach." One method is to check on AASI accreditation. This refers to the American Association of Snowboard Instructors, a national organization which certifies its members in levels of accomplishment not only in terms of skill at snowboarding, but more importantly to the resort guest, the organization evaluates teaching techniques and understanding of the sport's technology. All of this means that if you see a bronze colored Level I pin, you know that the instructor is associated. If a silver Level II jacket pin, the person has passed a three day exam testing technological understanding, teaching, and riding ability. With the Level III gold comes recognition of the highest accreditation in the mastering of the organization's standards. At least the awareness of AASI offers you some guide as to competence, and professionalism. The better your instructor, the more you will learn, and the more confident and capable you will become.

The point of this chapter is **not** to imply that you should not snowboard because of fear of injury but rather to allay fears by confronting the reality that sports involve risks. You will certainly be safer sitting home, but is that really what life is all about? Being with friends or family is certainly more stimulating than sitting staring at a television screen in physical and emotional isolation. Snowboarding offers an escape from everyday matters with the excitement of getting away. It brings you out with people, providing a socially interactive experience. Its outdoor activity refreshes and invigorates your life. All of these positive factors far outweigh the negatives of injury risk, especially when the latter is, to a very great extent, within your control. Accidents happen, but people do tend to play a role in causing them. Safety awareness and caution are keys to returning home happy and injury free.

QUESTION:

THERE ARE FOUR SNOWBOARDERS IN A CAR. WHO'S THE DRIVER?

ANSWER:

A POLICE OFFICER

CHAPTER 3
HOW TO LOOK THE LOOK

This is an important chapter. Don't just dismiss it as a fashion statement guide. Wearing snowboard specific clothing may be key to first day success on the slopes. If you are dressed improperly, you will either be sweaty and clammy, or cold and miserable, or all of the above. In the sport of snowboarding, although people may appear casually dressed without the sleek matched outfits of a skier, such impromptu looks may be deceptive. Actually, their clothing has usually been very specifically chosen. Follow these suggestions for clothing selection, and you will not only last out the lesson dry, warm, and in comfort but also enjoy it more. Although you can rent the board and boots at the mountain, what you wear must be carefully thought out and obtained in advance.

You surely are aware that snowboarders in their loose baggy clothes have a different style of dress from skiers. This is because, particularly when learning, you will be very actively using your entire body and, as a result, even on a cold day, often working up a sweat. In fact, when I teach a beginner group we sometimes have to make a clothing pile on the side of the trail as people become so overheated that it is necessary to strip off some of those unnecessary layers. On the other hand, the opposite clothing problem may arise in clinic groups when chattering teeth indicate that there has not been the best choice made in clothing selection. Whether being damp with sweat from being overheated or chilled because you are not warm enough, there is a way to dress which prepares you in either case. This chapter will deal with how the body actually processes temperature adjustments along with suggestions for appropriate clothing product selections.

Since most of the snowboard season is when temperatures are low, one must dress accordingly. I teach in Vermont which is known for its cold winters, but winter is winter. Just because you are going out west does not mean it will always be warm. Don't be thrown off by the magazine ads which picture bright sunshine . If it's cold enough to maintain snow, then it's usually fairly cold (except for spring conditions which usually occur in late March or April). The various factors to be considered are temperature, wind chill, amount of sunshine, time of day, and where you plan to be on the mountain.

Basic Premise

There are two aspects of dressing for the cold which are often not known to the novice. The first involves headgear. The easiest way to explain the importance of wearing a hat is that you should think of your body as a house, and your head is the chimney. If your head is uncovered, all the heat will rise straight up out of your body! It is as simple as that. If you are cold, put on a hat; if you wish to be warm, wear a hat. Note that "hat" does not mean "headband" which only protects your ears and does not prevent body heat loss. While on the subject, a better choice than a hat is that of a helmet. If helmets are worn for biking, motorcycling, and in-line skating, then why not for snowboarding? The advantages of the helmet are many (see Chapter 2). Aside from the safety factor, they really keep you incredibly warm even on the coldest days. Also, there is the added bonus that they are totally cool in terms of snowboarding fashion. They make you look as if you know what you are doing out there.

Often people complain that it's not their head that gets cold but it's the hands and feet. Not what you think! First of all, snowboard boots are warm. But the more pertinent answer to this problem of extremities involves the second aspect of winter dressing. The savvy snowsport person knows that hands and feet get cold because the body's circulatory system has gone into emergency mode. Because your heat is presumably going out of that open chimney of the no-hat head, the kidneys have sent out an alert signal. The circulatory system draws the blood from the extremities to help warm the body trunk, leaving fingers and toes numb with cold. Put on a warm hat or helmet, grab an extra layer for your upper body, and your toes will stay warm.

The other element to be considered is the fact that snowboarding involves a physical workout. As stated earlier, even on a cold day, you will perspire. If you are wearing the wrong kind of undergarments, that sweat will stay as a layer of moisture soaking your clothing, leaving you cold and uncomfortable. You could be wearing a really warm jacket but no matter how the manufacturer has convinced you of the quality of this outerwear product, you must still take further precautions to be amply warm. Those are the theories of dressing. Now for some specifics.

On Layering

The art of layering is based upon the theory that body heat is sandwiched and insulated between the various layers of clothing thereby creating little pockets of warm air. Because of today's high technology fabrics, the layering need not be cumbersome; thin fabrics, if they are the right kind, do the job without bulking you up. Anyway, as a snowboarder there is no problem fitting multiple layers underneath because of our baggy style of outerwear.

Underwear: First Layer

The first purchase you must make is for a set of long underwear made of any of those new fabrics which, as their advertising states, "wick away body moisture." The buzzword is "moisture transport." Get that sweat off your body. Damp clothing will not make your day glorious. It will make you feel clammy, be smelly, and certainly not contribute towards having a good day out there. Nobody wears wool anymore. It's not only itchy but also stays damp. Cotton absorbs and holds the moisture, another poor choice. To insure the fact that you are not going to be cold from body moisture soaked undergarments, look for items made from moisture wicking fabric, which usually go under designations of "polypropylene" tagged with vocabulary such as "moisture permeable," "bi-ply," "wicking," *etc.* The various manufacturers seem to have their own names for their individually registered trademarked materials. DuPont's "Cool-Max," Patagonia's "Capilene," Burton's "DryRide," Medalist's "comFortel,"DuPont's "DuoFold Vent-A-Layer" made of "ThermaStat,"and "MicroFiber One are just a few of the many choices. These are really great products with unique hydrophobic (water rejecting) abilities. Their technology allows channel fibers to move moisture away from the skin and therefore will keep you comfortably dry.

You should wear a first layer, top and bottom, made of one of these high tech fabrics. One can even do a second layer of fleece for bitter super cold days. There are so many new high quality products out there. Check out items from Patagonia Company (they offer 6 different weights of layering underwear), Burton, L.L. Bean, Eddie Bauer, and of course, don't overlook your local ski/snowboarding shop's inventory. In fact, the latter mentioned ski shops along with Patagonia and Burton will have the best choices since they are entirely focused on outdoor sport clothing, whereas L.L. Bean and Eddie Bauer are more diverse in their offerings and can't really compare in terms of depth of snowboard-specific selection. Read those labels and select wisely. For those who like to do virtual shopping, be sure to check out the listings at the end of this chapter.

Turtleneck Shirt

After that first layer of polypropylene, then wear one of those high tech material blend turtleneck shirts. This keeps the neck area warm. For those who hate tight neckwear, there are companies who make zipper necks. If it is really cold out, I prefer to wear fleece. Again, cotton is a no-no.

Sweater

Next would come a sweater, either wool, acrylic, or fleece. Historically, ski sweaters were those bulky knits which were heavy weight so one presumed that they were exceedingly warm; however, it's the layering which creates and holds the warmth, not the heavy weight of the knit. Size is not too crucial, as the bigger the better to use for layering over that turtleneck and long underwear top. Color is not so important; snowboarders are truly not inhibited by fashion color coordinates. Leave that cool looking sweatshirt back in the hotel room for evening social wear; it won't be the right garb for on the mountain (remember: avoid cotton!).

Some companies, such as Ibex (www.ibexwear.com) have even improved upon wool, using technology to improve insulation from dampness and wind. Smartwool (www.smartwool.com) uses Merino wool which is constructed to keep you warm, not damp, and not bulky. Another handy item is a fleece vest as it warms the central body organs without bulk around the arms. Or instead, a fleece pullover shirt goes perfectly on top of that thin sweater or in place of it. Fleece has an added advantage in that it is machine washable so it is an easy care item.

Variation in Dress for Extreme Cold: Brrrrr

Actually, it is only really bitter cold in midwinter. This is true out west along with the northeast regions. The coldest temperature I have ever experienced on a ski trip was in Steamboat, Colorado, early in February. In fact, it was so cold that the mountain had been closed the previous week. Therefore, for January or February, it is usually necessary to consider supplementing the layering process I have mentioned when dressing for near or sub zero temperatures taking into account the additional influencing factors of wind chill and lack of sunshine. On the bottoms, over the moisture wicking first layer comes a second of fleece. Remember that although you may have a warmer jacket to protect your upper body, usually one's wardrobe is limited to a single pair of snowboard pants, whatever the weight. Upper body warmth is easier. Just pile on the various layers, with fleece as the best fabric choice.

Jacket

There have been many articles and even a book written on the subject of "choice" with the finding that when one is faced with too many choices, the tendency is not to make any decision at all. Too many products lead to confusion, and that is what faces you with the racks of jackets in a typical snowboard shop. Many are products from start up companies, but there are those which have been out there standing the test of time and moving forward in design as the sport of snowboarding has developed. Any list of the leading companies of snowboard specific outerwear would include the following: Arc'teryx, Bonfire, Burton, Helly Hansen, K2, Nike, Quicksilver, Rip Curl, Ride, Sessions, and Volcom. There may be others, but those are certainly among the most popular and are choices I would recommend for you to help narrow the field of decision making.

Thirty years ago the only waterproof breathable fabric on the market was the new (and expensive) invention of Gore-Tex. Today there are so very many fabrics out there that it's virtually impossible to list them all properly. The main thing to keep in mind is that when reading the labels check to see words such as "breathable" and know the direction of your concern which is to move water vapor (produced by body perspiration) outward. This is *breathability* as opposed to *waterproofing* which prevents water from coming inward. Remember, unless you plan to spend a lot of time riding on rainy days, it is basically the seat of a snowboarder's pants where waterproofing is most necessary and most appreciated.

Choose your jacket carefully, as snowboarding jackets differ from those of skiers. Their design is more functional in that this sport involves upper body movement which means that loose fitting cuts and pit zip venting offer comfort while the longer length allows one to bend over to make binding adjustments without having the jacket hike up to your waist. Lots of pockets are always a bonus to stash away bulky stuff like sunglasses or goggles.

In case you may wonder why I have devoted so much attention to the first and middle clothing layers, and so little to this third outermost layer, it is because today's snowboard specific jackets are so well designed to meet the demands of the sport that, applying my brand list, you won't need a lot of guidance here. Watch for zip off hoods, venting systems, water repellant fabrics, and ample pockets. It's possible to look good along with practicality.

Remember to check breathability. Plastic is totally waterproof, but it certainly wouldn't be a good idea for a snowboard jacket! Hence, waterproof is not the prime desirable factor. These new fabrics offer weather protection, warmth in trapping body heat, and breathability so that body moisture is not trapped inside. Some products are now even advertising outerwear which absorbs the warmth of the sun and conversely releases excessive body heat outward.

The technology is charging ahead so very fast, in fact, that there recently appeared an article in *The Wall Street Journal* on the development of a water resistant outdoor jacket equipped with a built-in player for music downloaded from the Internet, a cell phone, headset, and a remote control. We are growing accustomed to seeing skiers and snowboarders on cell phones and many favor the use of walkie-talkie transceivers, but the era of wearable electronics is soon to be upon us. There will be shirts with speakers and solar panels on outerwear for body warmth along with solar rechargeable jackets to act as batteries for all that built in equipment.

Pants

Skiers can stand still because they have poles to stabilize them. The snowboarder, when stopped, unless the surface is really flat, will be more comfortable when sitting down. The problem is that sitting means that you are on a surface of wet snow and often for extended periods of time. Therefore, it is really important to wear the right kind of outerwear pants. Forget about jeans. They are actually like blotters, attracting and absorbing water. Water resistant pants are simply a MUST. Look at the design of many snowboard pants, and you will see that they often have inserted a heavy (waterproof) section on the seat offering added protection from the snow.

Another thing to look for when purchasing snowboard pants are built in pockets inside at the knee for (foam) pads. Not absolutely necessary, but a nice feature. When not sitting in the snow, one is kneeling on the snow. Knees get cold, wet, and sometimes battered. External knee pads are fine, but inside pads are more subtle and comfortable, definitely a bonus. Remember when in the store trying on pants that while snowboarding you would have on at least one layer of long underwear underneath and sometimes an additional layer of fleece, so be sure that the waistline is ample. Lately, the two most popular styles are both cargo and carpenter pants which each offer the bonus of extra pockets. Beware, however; if you have items stashed away there such as car keys, you might find an imprint of them on your leg as a result of rolling over. A well situated pocket is the one down at the hem line by the bottom cuff. It's the perfect place for your cell phone or keys.

Side zips on pant legs allowing for venting are absolutely on top of the list as a desirable option come spring temps.

Socks

For your feet, there are simple do's and don'ts. **Do not** wear multiple socks. This will only restrict your blood circulation. In most cases a rental arrangement will result in your being outfitted with "soft" snowboard boots (not the hard style which looks like a ski boot). These are well insulated and will definitely keep your feet nice and warm. **Do not** borrow boots and plan on wearing several layers of socks to improve the boot fit. **Do** wear a good cushioned athletic sock.

Neck Gaiter

Another element of clothing which will certainly make your day outside more pleasant is the neck gaiter. This is simply an oversize fleece turtleneck and sold in all ski shops. Lightweight and not bulky, you can easily stash it away onto the shoulder area of your jacket sleeve and whip it out for use later if you are cold. This will keep your neck and lower face warm and covered. Long scarves may look dashing but are really not a good idea as one runs the risk of becoming entangled when riding on a lift. Face masks? These used to be called balaclavas, made of wool or a similar knitted fabric. Along with looking like a possible bank robber, they tend to freeze up from breath moisture. The neoprene ones now on the market do a much better job.

Gloves and mittens.

No matter what the advertisers say about the waterproof

quality of their gloves and mittens, they always seem to soak through rather quickly when snowboarding. That's because you are using them to wipe the binding plate clear of loose snow and also due to the fact that you spend so much time sitting down with your hands on snow. Those specifically designed for snowboarding sometimes are more water resistant than the ski variety due to an understanding of the snowboarder's excessive contact with snow surface. My advice is to bring two pairs and plan to change at lunchtime.

Mittens keep fingers warmer than gloves as they allow for mutual warmth, but the downside is that it is harder to negotiate bindings when wearing mittens compared to gloves. One way to keep fingers toasty warm, whether with gloves or mittens, is to purchase those little heat packs (sold at ski shops). Simply shake to activate, then set them inside. You will feel as if you've ignited a miniature furnace which provides heat throughout the day. According to Grabber My Coal Hand Warmers (telephone 800-423-1233), you "get exothermic" (whatever that means). Glove liners also work well, adding an insulating layer. An advantage of the latter is that if you must remove a mitten to make a binding adjustment, your hand is protected from the cold by the glove liner which is usually of silk or polyester knit.

Goggles and Sunglasses.

Proper eye protection is a high priority item when outdoors in the mountain environment. One tends to think of eye covering in regard to filtering the rays of the sun, but here the situation is more complex. Not only is the sun stronger in high altitudes where there is less oxygen, but there is the additional element of glaring sunlight reflected off of the snow surface. Dermatologist have made us well aware of the fact that even on cloudy days, the rays of the sun filter through. While on the mountain there is the additional need to protect your eyes from wind and snow.

In cold weather skiers and snowboarders wear goggles rather than sunglasses because they are physically larger and therefore play a protective role in helping cover skin area otherwise exposed to the elements. One should plan on wearing goggles throughout the winter season when there is less sun and the days are shorter. The preferred color lens for that time of year would be amber or pink, either of which works well in flat light situations. Add a neck gaiter and wind guard face cream, and you will be ready for those cold gusts of wind which tend to arrive late in the day when the sun goes under cloud cover.

The bright sunlight of spring comes with warmer temperatures, so one should then opt for sunglasses. Preferable are the wrap around shaped frames which act as a wind screen for the side areas of the eye, particularly suitable for contact lens wearers. There are some lenses out on the market which change degree of darkness in accordance with the brightness of the sunlight, adding still another choice.

Miscellaneous Accessories

Lock

This should be the first item on your accessories list. It's a really good idea to have a ski/ snowboard lock, whether purchased or borrowed from a ski friend. Not every ski area has a snowboard check facility where, for a slight fee, you can leave your board (you are not allowed to bring snowboards into the lodge). Although you may be renting your snowboard, you are still responsible for it, and they do get stolen with rather alarming frequency.

Face Cream

Face creams are not just for women. Creams are a necessity for skiers and boarders in prevention of exposure to cold, sleet and snow, windburn, sunburn, and especially frostbite. Sold at ski areas, these are special creams which offer protection from the elements. It is sort of a joke among skiers in Vermont that locals know to use Bag Balm to protect their skin from excessive cold. This is an antiseptic ointment much like a very heavy Vaseline and is used by farmers to coat the teats of milk cows, protecting this tender area. Although one can sometimes find small containers in the local Vermont convenience store, it is usually sold in giant size tins, enough to last you throughout your snowboarding career. They do not seem to have a web site, but you can write to the Dairy Association Company, Inc., Lydonville, Vermont 05851. I recently noticed that my local CVS drug store was carrying this product.

A disadvantage of Bag Balm is its lack of protection from the sun. In fact, it seems to induce sunburn. Instead, for sunny days one should consider any of the regular sun screen products you would use during the summer at the beach or check out the various creams sold at ski shops such as the products from Dermatone. This company's line has a variety of items such as sun screen lotion offering total protection from the sun with a zinc SPF of 36, a stick protector of SPF 23 for sun, wind and cold, lip balm, and a handy "mini tin"of cream which offers multiple protection from frostbite, wind, and also the sun.

As already cautioned, the sun poses a serious problem with its direct rays plus snow reflection. At the western resorts there is the additional problem of high altitude sunburn. Be really careful. You will quickly learn that warm weather riding presents extra precautions because when not wearing a hat your ears and even the area where your hair parts may become severely sunburned. Even though you are packing for a winter trip, it's a good idea to remember to search your out of season items and find that container of sunscreen.

Ditty Pack

Ski lodges have basket checks or lockers (bring plenty of quarters) where you can stash extra items such as spare mittens, sweaters and fleece vests. Skiers have an advantage in the wearing of fanny packs, those zip pouches worn about the waist. The problem with such an accessory for the snowboarder is that in case of a fall, you will receive an impression onto your spinal cord of each stowed item, and it can prove quite painful. Backpacks look somewhat absurd. You are going snowboarding, not hiking. I actually insist that my clinic participants not wear backpacks as the weight throws off a person's natural body posture. It is hard enough for a beginner to balance on a snowboard. Adding an unnatural body weight makes it virtually impossible.

The best solution is (1) take only necessities which fit into your pockets or (2) while in a ski/snowboard shop ask the clerk about a "ditty pack" which is basically a wallet worn on a cord which hangs from your neck. There is enough room for cash, car keys, credit card, *etc.* and you won't risk having things fall out of a tightly stuffed pocket. I have brought to the Lost and Found desk numerous cell phones and car keys. It's easy to be distracted into leaving one of those many jacket pockets unzipped, and snowboarding certainly involves many active movements which increases the chance of loss of balance along with the resultant loss of pocket objects.

Hydration Pack

This is a relatively newer accessory which is appearing for mountain use, particularly out west or during spring season in the east, in either case when dehydration is a serious problem. Sold at ski, snowboard, and also bike shops, products are available from companies such as Safe Water whose web-site is www.safewateranywhere.com, or Platypus at www.cascadedesigns.com, Ultimate Direction www.ultimatedirection.com, Camelbak www.camelbak.com, or try the compact Micro-Stash from Backcountry Access, www.bcaccess.com. All of these companies have created water carriers which allow snowboarders to easily hydrate while riding. The advertisement for Camelbak has a heavy duty warning which you should heed: "Hydrate or die!"

"Jewelry"

One last admonition-- for my body pierced friends. If you have ever tried pouring hot liquid into a tin container which you are holding, you are well aware that metal conducts heat. You need not take advanced science laboratory courses to know that the same transfer occurs with cold temperatures. Your exposed body rings will transfer the degree of cold to your skin and thereby increase the danger of frostbite. I always keep close watch on my body-pierced snowboarding students who have rings in noses, eyebrows, or other such weather exposed skin. Be a good snowboarding buddy, and act as a mirror for your friends in keeping a lookout for incipient frostbite in these areas. See Chapter 9 for details on frostbite, how to identify it, and what to do for it.

Communication Devices

The use of "talkabouts"is now ubiquitous at most ski areas. These are those hand held radios which people use on the mountain to converse with their friends as a handy way to locate each other. Because the many channels are usually kept quite busy, conversations are mostly limited to discussions of which lodge, lift, or trail the separate parties are at and where they can meet. Cell phones are also good items to carry in that they can be used for emergency situations. Rather than calling 911, you should dial the mountain resort and request ski patrol help. The only problem with both of these communication devices aside from reception difficulties is that first, you will need sufficient pocket room for storage, and secondly, you will have to take off your warm mittens to hit those tiny keys. Also, having a telephone with you means that you really haven't escaped from your cares. Who wants to be receiving telephone calls when you're out there having fun?

❄ ❄ ❄ ❄ ❄

Hopefully, this rather exhaustive discussion has neither intimidated nor discouraged you. It is simply much easier to know in advance what you will need rather than arrive at the mountain and find out the hard way that you are inadequately dressed or supplied. Most towns have ski/snowboard shops which have good selections, and with the Internet one has extensive shopping options. There's always the opportunity to pick up needed equipment at a ski area where one usually has the best possible selection of items (although who wants to waste *apres ski* party time by going shopping?). You can always borrow, which reminds me: **A Household Hint**. If you have opted to resurrect a jacket or pants from your past skiing history or have borrowed such clothing, you can do the following to freshen the quality of its water repellence. Wash using powder not liquid detergent. After drying, apply a water repelling spray such as Scotch-Gard.

What to Wear Summary (trip packing list)

The forecast is for partly sunny weather, windy, high in the mid-twenties. Wear the following:

on top:

- polypropylene undershirt
- polypropylene or blend turtleneck shirt
- sweater or fleece
- take along a fleece vest (just in case)
- outerwear jacket

on bottom:

- polypropylene long underwear blend bottoms
- socks
- snowboard pants

other items to bring along:

- two pairs mittens/gloves
- neck gaiter
- hat and helmet
- face cream, sun protection cream
- goggles, sunglasses

ski lock
ditty pack

After a Day on the Slopes

This is the well known *apres ski* time when all gather to discuss the day's successes or misadventures. Clothing suggestions? Blue jeans seem to be the universal choice. Once the sun goes down, temperatures drop. This is the situation where I find that silk long underwear to be perfect as an added layer under those cotton jeans. Yes, they make silk underwear for men; check the LL Bean catalog. Silk adds a layer of warmth and does not take up any appreciable space. Since there are no sidewalks and everything is snow covered, be sure that you have packed snow boots or sturdy waterproof shoes. Leave the sneakers at home as they are wicked slippery on wet surfaces.

Spring Conditions

All of the above is fine for New England resorts and winter months, but March and April bring milder weather, particularly in the Rockies. European winters (and South America during our summers) are also warmer. I have memories of skiing wearing a bathing suit top while skiing in the afternoon yet needing a down parka at night in April at Jackson Hole, Wyoming. The main thing to remember when packing for those climes is the danger of high altitude sunburn along with dehydration during the day, and the fact that, no matter what the season, it gets quite cold at night in the mountains. You might be wearing a wind shirt during the day, but you will definitely need that warm parka at night.

The rules for dressing are basically the same as for cold

weather except for lighter weight selections: long underwear which wicks away perspiration, turtleneck, thin waterproof jacket or wind shirt, waterproof pants and of course, never ever wear cotton. Spring snowboard clothing usually is constructed with zipped underarms on jackets or zippered leg sides on pants which provide venting. Be sure to wear gloves. Lightweight clothing not only protects you from the sun but also from the snow. If you happen to fall, the snow is like sandpaper, and the abrasion will be painful on unprotected skin.

Head coverings, in general, trap the heat. You can wear a lightweight beany style hat or baseball cap (remember to bring a baseball cap tie-clip to prevent its flying off while riding). Headgear is necessary to protect your scalp and ears from sunburn. Fortunately, most helmets now are designed with warm weather vents which are quite effective.

Sun screen is a must, even for your lip balm. A handy piece of equipment are the hydration packs already mentioned. Dehydration is a problem when on the mountain (particularly in the high altitudes) and easily leads to fatigue, headache, and loss of energy. Leave the fleece clothing at home except do bring something warm for evening wear. I always wonder about the people sitting next to me on a chairlift when the weather is a balmy 50 + degrees, and they are bundled in down jackets. I guess they reasoned that if there is snow on the slopes, then it must be cold out. Not always true.

Rain

For springtime conditions, remember to pack a raincoat. In cold weather it snows, but when temperatures rise, there's rain. Altitude also has bearing on the weather. At Whistler-Blackcomb in British Columbia, Canada, although it can be raining at the lower area of the mountain, it most likely will be snowing in the upper regions. By the way, snowboarding in the rain is just wonderful. The crowds are sitting indoors at the lodge which means that the trails will be empty of people, and the snow quality tends to be really super. It can be lots of fun, that is **if** you are toasty warm and dry. One important precaution: damp moist air takes away body heat faster than dry air, leaving one vulnerable to chills or even hypothermia. Therefore, although the temperature may be relatively warm, you should remember to dress as if it's actually a bit colder on those damp days.

Appendix : Products and Where to Find Them

I mentioned the importance of reading labels, but it's not really quite as simple as that. The problem can be twofold: where to find the clothing items in the first place and the fact that each company seems to have a different name for their special "wicking" fabric. Hopefully, the following very limited listing (in no particular order) will be of some help to you in dealing with this quandary.

Patagonia

www.patagonia.com This is a company which specializes in rugged outdoor sportswear. Go to their online store and select "Shop by Sport" then select " Skiing and Boarding" and select "Men's."You will undergo a full education on the movement of moisture through fabric. Their high performance underwear, referred to as "Patagonia Phundamentals," is made of a material which they have developed called "Capilene." There are various products, and the ones you would be interested in would be the Silkweight Stretch (note that silk only refers to the weight, not the fabric), the denser moisture wicking Midweight for greater warmth, or their well known Expedition Weight which is of a super warm fleece. The web site also explains the concept of layering in three defined zones: Innermost Layer (the moisture wicking fabrics), Insulating Layer (your discretionary decision as to fleece or sweaters), and Outer Layer (jacket or shell).

Burton

Their product line is so extensive that the company publishes a separate catalog just for men. You can go to Burton various ways, either online at www.burton.com , by calling 800-881-3138 to request a catalog, or by seeing the items in person at a quality ski/snowboard shop in your area (check the yellow pages). A pioneer in the industry with their company based in Vermont, the gear is primarily designed for rugged winters. There's a full line of what they refer to as "First Layer Core Weight" items of their Dry Ride 100% polyester or microfleece underwear in both midweight and expedition weight. Their years of expertise produce products which are "rider-designed for snowboard-specific performance."

K2

Washington state is at the very opposite coast of the United States from Vermont and the home of K2, another company early involved in the development of snowboarding. Going online at www.k2snowboards.com puts you in touch, and their product guide catalog pictures the wide selection of outerwear (along with the expected listings of equipment and accessories), all very specifically designed for our sport. Again, look in your local ski/snowboard shop for these excellent products.

Sessions

Sessions is a company which traces its roots (and designing spirit) to skateboarding, snowboarding, surfing and also punk rock. Go to the web site www.sessions.com and be entertained by a slide show of the company history. They are on my list for jacket choice.

Volcom

This name also is on my listing of jackets. They are makers of quality clothing and the web site www.volcom.com not only goes over their outerwear products and company history, but it also is a great site in terms of all sorts of informative happenings. They explain and give details about programs such as Let the Kids Ride Free or the Peanut Butter and Rail Jam amateur snowboard series. They even have an art gallery with requests for submissions.

Helmets

You can't properly purchase a helmet without first trying it on because size is crucial. Heads vary, and a poorly fitting helmet will not only give you a headache but also shortchange you on protection value and even increase your chance of injury. Check for lightweight comfort, good hearing ability, ventilation (they can be very hot in the warmer weather and by then you will be addicted to wearing them), and style as there is variety among the many companies.

According to *Skiing* magazine, the first criteria is that one should definitely only consider a helmet which has passed one of the three safety standards: CE, ASTM, or Snell. The next things to evaluate are that it should allow good visibility, not be too tight, and yet be snug enough not to slide around when you move your head up and down. A loose helmet can cause serious neck injury.

Snowboarders tend to wear the "shorty" versions, but really, anything goes. Some popular companies and their sites to check out on the web are Salomon at www.salomonsports.com, Boeri at www.boeriusa.com, Giro at www.giro.com, Carrera at www.carrerasport.com, and Briko at www.briko.com. By far and away, however, the best overall web site to check out is www.lidsonkids.org which will help educate you on the entire subject. Although the name suggests orientation for helmet use by children, there is a great deal of general and very useful information posted here. The web site was developed by the National Ski Areas Association, National Ski Patrol, Professional Ski Instructors of America, American Association of Snowboard Instructors, International Brain Injury Association, National Safety Council, and Snowsports Industries America, and is sponsored by Acerbis USA, Boeri, Giro, Leedom, Ovo USA, R.E.D., Salomon, and W Helmets. Need I say more?

Goggles or Sunglasses

Goggle selection closely follows helmet choice. **Be sure that you are wearing your helmet when selecting goggles.** Otherwise, they simply might not fit. As stated earlier, there is a fairly wide choice of lens color which therefore may require some degree of analysis. According to the Bolle company, Vermillon, their high contrast rose lens is for cloudy/overcast conditions. I find that this lens is excellent in the flat light of late afternoon or on snowy midwinter days. Their Citrus orange is for bright light (sunny) days; Lemon, a yellow, is for low light. Clear lenses are usually only used for night skiing. A single choice could be Phototropic which goes from light amber to dark, depending upon the amount of sunlight.

One might be tempted to purchase one set of goggles with several varied colors of replacement lenses. The problem with this route in terms of my personal experience is that it is not really quite so easy to substitute a lens without cracking it. Goggle replacement lenses are really on the market for when you have to do just that: replace a broken lens, not to do a quick switch based on weather conditions. Investigate the following sites on the web: www.bolle.com, www.briko.com, www.scott.com, www.carrerasport.com, www.vuarnet.com, www.smith.com, www.gordini.com, www.oakley.com, www.bugz.com, www.spy.com. Because your helmet will hold in body warmth, you should select goggles which have vents, the more vents, the better. Most have top vents, but with helmet usage, the additional front vents make a substantial difference in avoiding fogging. Goggles should fit snugly, and be sure that the strap fits properly over the helmet and holds into place.

Sunglasses should also be tried on with your helmet to be sure of a comfortable fit. Contact lens users should select frames which either have a wrap around design or have side extending shields, in either case to protect from wind. Look for quality lenses that are shatterproof and will allow you to be out there with full u.v. protection and no squinting. Polarized lenses help cut the harsh glare of sunlight which is amplified by its reflection off of the snow. As with the goggles, some companies even have sunglasses with interchangeable lenses. www.bolle.com, www.zealoptics.com, www.nerveusa.com. , www.oakley.com, www.serengeti.com, www.carrerasport.com, and www.briko.com, are just some of the choices. Select the right lens color. Although they look really cool and funky, those yellow, pink, or red are for low light cloudy conditions. Practically speaking, however, because goggles offer the advantage of wind and cold protection, sunglasses are usually reserved for warmer weather which means that it is usually bright and sunny, so choose your lens color accordingly.

Remember that unlike the fashion market for street wear, in snowsports country the price is your best indication of lens quality and impact protection.

Socks

I have already mentioned the importance of wearing a good athletic sock and recommend the Thorlo company which makes different socks for a variety of sporting activities, including snowboarding. Their snowboard sock has cushioning in just the right places: www.thorlo.com or call 888 t-h-o-r-l-o-s for the nearest retailer.

Ski Barn

I live in the New York metropolitan area, and the shop which I go to the most is the Ski Barn, on the web at www.skibarn.com or you can visit any one of their three New Jersey stores (Lawrenceville, Paramus, or Totowa) in person. I have been going to the Totowa store for many years because of their selection of goods and very knowledgeable staff. In fact, I have attended the company's training sessions where staff learns (on snow) about all of the newest product lines for the upcoming season. There's a lot to know to be a savvy salesperson; it requires personal experience with the equipment plus an understanding of the technology. These are qualities to look for to determine where you shop and what you will purchase.

Pelican Sport Center and High Country Sports

New Jersey has many ski clubs and consequently many good shops. Check out Pelican Sport Center, located on Rt. 10 West in Morris Plains, telephone 973-267-0964 or www.pelicanski.com. Same road, another town and an excellent destination is High Country Sports, 465 Route 10 East, Livingston,973-994-3630, www.hcsports.com

LL Bean, REI, E.M.S.

Their web site, www.llbean.com ,offers a full range of catalog items. However, if you go to the "sporting gear and apparel," "men's sporting apparel," and proceed to then select "skiing & snowboarding," although there are items listed, they certainly are not as technically presented such as with any ski/snowboard shop or compared to, for example, Patagonia. I do recommend, however, the L.L. Bean 100% silk underwear which I mentioned for under jeans in mountain climes. These are perfect to wear not when snowboarding, but, instead, when walking around the ski resort *apres ski* as the sun goes down and temperatures quickly drop. The reason why one would not want to wear silk underwear while riding is because silk fabric does not breathe. You would be very uncomfortable.

The list of resources goes on and on, such as the web

sites for REI (www.rei.com), and for E.M.S. (www.easternmountainsports.com). Certainly, there are other sources available as this book is being written, and more to come, but this will hopefully be a helpful starting point for you.

Resort Area Snowboard Shops

In truth, almost all of my equipment purchases are made either, as already stated, at my local ski shop in New Jersey where I live or at my resort where I also have a home. I work at Killington where the company ski stores are Chrisports Ski Shops at the mountain lodge areas and Shops at the Shack, all carrying very high quality goods. That's a bonus situation as there is always something you may have forgotten to bring to the mountain. Convenience and selection are additional points to be considered here.

Along with the company stores, I recommend several of my local Killington snowboard shops: Out of Bounds snowboard shop, www.ridevt.com, or First Stop-Board Barn at www.info@firststopski.com. The advantage of these ski area shops is that they can devote their stock exclusively to handling only snowboarding products. If you know what you want, it's just a matter of finding the shop with that specific item in its inventory. Really, the very best way to shop is in person so that you can try on things, and the very best place to shop is either at your home located specialty ski/snowboard shop or even better, at those of your destination resort which has the additional advantage of your being able to try out the product right there, on the spot.

There is one problem with ski area shopping which is that although the resort stores may be numerous and usually excellent, including, as the case at Killington, those run by the ski area itself, however, a person simply has limited time (and energy) to go shopping after a day on the slopes. But, this is a great place to pick up exactly the item you have been seeking, that is if you have the strength to muster up for the shopping expedition. It's not the snowboarding lesson itself that is so tiring but the use of new muscles plus the day long exposure to the outdoors. It can be exhausting.

Which source did I forget? Perhaps the biggest and the best!

An indefatigable resource is www.snowlink.com which really is the penultimate source for all listings. Here you will find the web sites for equipment, clothing, resort information, snowsport articles, weather reports for resort areas, lesson information, just about everything you never even thought you could have wanted to know.

QUESTION:

HOW DO YOU GET A SNOWBOARDER OUT OF YOUR CLOSET?

ANSWER:

CHARGE HIM RENT.

CHAPTER 4
HOW TO TALK THE TALK

Snowboarding is more than just another snowsport. It differs from skiing, snowblading, and telemark in that it loudly and clearly proclaims a certain attitude. Growing out of skateboarding and surfing, snowboarding has always identified itself somewhat as a youth oriented counter culture activity despite the growing number of skiers who have crossed over to boarding plus the fact that more and more adults are becoming shredders. Neither has drastically changed the image, although now, with its recent attainment of status as an Olympic sport, there is much more of a cross-generational appeal. I have given numerous parent-child shared lessons, once even extended to three generations with grandparent, child, and grandchild all learning together.

Although age is no barrier, one must communicate, and snowboarders certainly do tend to speak their own special language. There is the technical vocabulary which obviously you should know, but there is also a full glossary of words which you will *want* to know, such as, for a start, "rad dude" because that's YOU!

These are not in alphabetical order, mostly because they are listed in the order of what I think you will find more of interest. Anyway, this isn't a text book. Therefore, for example, if you don't really understand or care about the meaning of words like *sidecut* or *effective edge*, don't worry. That's why they are at the bottom of the list. Eventually, however, you'll want to know these technical terms.

The Lingo

rad dude *Rad* is short for radical meaning "extreme"and a *dude* is a guy. That's you.

betty The opposite sex: a *betty* is a gal who rides. That's me.

shred The word *shred* has sort of evolved in meaning. At first, years ago, it meant to snowboard, but then it went out of fashion, and amazingly was replaced in usage with the verb to ski (as in stating that you "have skied the trail",although the action was done on a board). Perhaps it was because so many snowboard instructors were also ski instructors. Lately the word *shred* has reappeared in usage , not only as a verb, *to go shredding* but also as an adjective to describe a person as a *shredhead* or as in the subtitle of my first book: *a guide for the Betty Shred wannabe.*

Yo! In Spanish this means "I" but to a snowboarder it's the standard greeting substitute for "Hello!"

stoked A person who is stoked is really excited about the riding experience.

dialed To be dialed is to be ready, eager to go. It actually originated as a reference to your binding being dialed in and set.

knuckle-dragger Get used to hearing this as it is what your skiing friends will call you.

hitch kicking This describes a sloppy turn move wherein the rider shoves the rear of the board into the turn rather than steering it to create a round turn shape.

360 Remember your geometry? There are 360 degrees in a circle; to do a 360 is to do a complete spin. A 180 is half a spin.

switch Riding your board in the opposite direction, backwards, used to be referred to as riding *fakie*, but that term is now out of fashion. The current description is "*riding switch.*"

freshies After a big dump, hurry out there to enjoy the *freshies* (fresh snow). When light and fluffy, it is also referred to as *pow,* short for powder.

big ups Thanks.

jibbing Riding over found objects such as fallen trees, handrails, or roof tops.

snowboarder's slam Unfortunately, all snowboarders tend to be initiated with this dreaded powerful thrust to the ground. It is caused by catching the board's downhill edge. Always be aware where is uphill when toeside or heelside, and be sure to stay to that side of the board for edging.

Words You *Should* Know

stance There are several components to stance as the term relates to whether you are regular, goofy or duck footed. It also refers to the angle degrees for each foot, the distance measured between the centers of each binding, binding placement relevant to tip and tail of the board, and also

	placement of binding between toe and heel edges.
regular	You ride regular if you have your left foot in the forward binding position.
goofy	This is a term derived from surfing which refers to having the right foot in the forward binding position on the board.
duck	The binding positions are pointing in opposite directions: front foot points to the board's nose while rear foot is directed towards the tail. The stance is reminiscent of the ballet toes-out position or "east-west" in the dog show ring.
stomp pad	This is an accessory placed on the snowboard just forward of the back foot binding. Its purpose is to create a non-slippery surface where your free foot is placed when getting off a lift.
leash	Lift operators will check your equipment to be sure that you have this strap to help prevent runaway boards. If a long strap, it wraps around the ankle area; if a hook, it connects to a boot lace.
nose	This is the front end of the board.
tail	The back end of the board.
skidding	A skidded turn is when the board moves forward while at the same time slipping sideways.
carving	A carved turn occurs when the board edge moves forward with minimal or no sideways slippage, leaving a clear cut line in the snow.
skating	This is how you propel the board forward,

pushing with the back foot which is out of its binding. One skates when entering and exiting a lift.

chatter You will feel a strong vibration coming from the board and impacting upon your body when experiencing *chatter.*

highback The highback is that vertical piece at the back part of the binding. Its purpose is to give support while turning heelside

fall line If a snowball were tossed onto the trail, it would roll down a path, the *fall line,* in the direction of the slope. There often will be more than one fall line such as when the trail goes downhill and at the same time also slopes sideways, making such terrain more challenging to ride.

traverse When learning to snowboard, one does not go straight downhill. Rather, one does a *traverse,* a directional movement across the trail rather than down the fall line.

retraction Stiff legs create a stiff ride. By bending your knees, *retracting* your legs, pulling them closer to your body, they help absorb the irregularities of the snow surface.

extension Extension is the opposite of retraction. Sudden extension can create an unweighting situation of lessened pressure on the board.

pivot This is a basic snowboarding movement which entails spinning around an axis in a rotational manner.

Some Tech Talk

deck This is the top sheet or upper surface of the snowboard, the place where you see the graphic design as you snowboard. Riders used to cover this area with stickers, but that has long gone out of style. Now it's just a place for bindings and stomp pad.

base This is the bottom sliding surface of the board where the graphic is coated with a layer of wax. The base, along with the metal edges, should receive constant attention in terms of good tuning maintenance.

length Given in centimeters, it is the measurement from nose to tail.

flex This is the relative stiffness of the board, how easily it bends. Flex is an important factor in relation to the weight and proficiency of the rider. There is *torsional flex* which refers to lateral twisting and *longitudinal flex* when bent from tip to tail.

waist The center area of the board, the *waist*, is usually the narrowest part. The *waist* width measurement is crucial in selecting a board for men who have a large boot size.

effective edge Even though the board has a specific length, not all of that distance ever touches the snow. The curved side or running edge (*sidecut*) is what actually traces the line of your turn and hence has an *effective* role.

sidecut Imagine a circle tracing the portion of the

outside curved edge of the board. Its radius is the radius of the *sidecut*. If this sounds complex, what it boils down to is that two boards may have the same length, but the amount of *sidecut* determines the *effective* edge, hence the turn radius.

camber This is the stored energy of a board, which makes it lively and responsive to your pressure. A great deal of *camber* requires quick turning; less is more "forgiving" and thus avoiding a slam. Lack of *camber* is akin to riding an old wooden plank.

sandwich The elements of snowboard are layered. For example, the fiberglass is used as the "lettuce" and the core is the "meat"in this order: base, fiberglass, wood or foam core, fiberglass, top. Edges are covered with a sidewall.

cap With this construction system, the upper fiberglass is not simply layered, but extends out and down the side edge, eliminating the necessity of a sidewall.

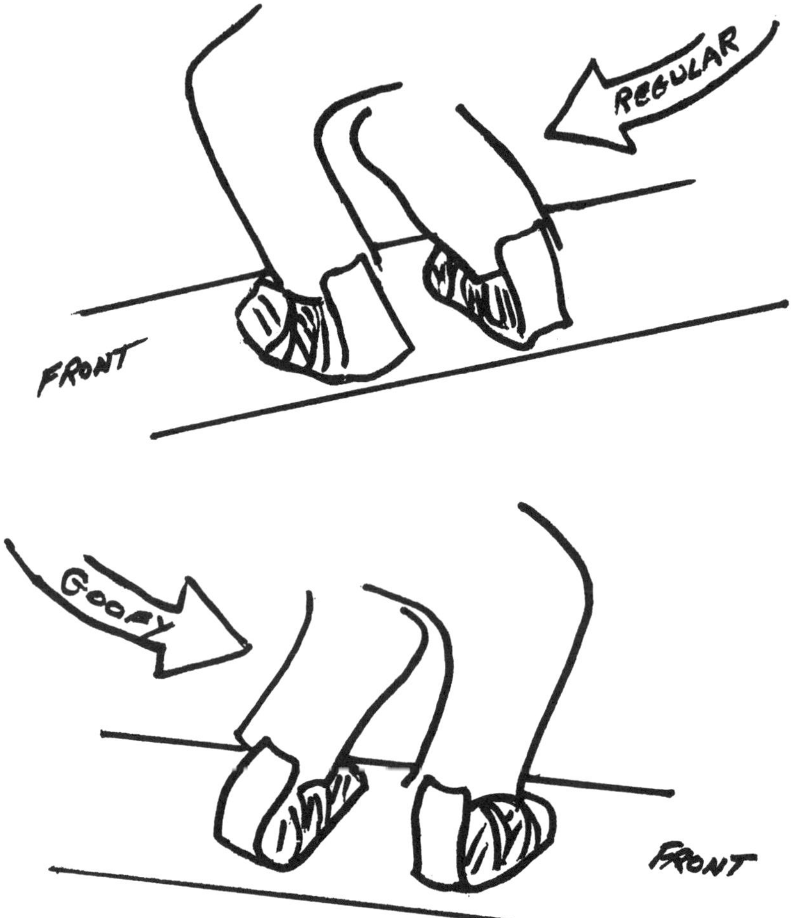
REGULAR
FRONT
GOOFY
FRONT

CHAPTER 5
HOW TO TAKE A STANCE

It's decided. You intend to snowboard, you have the proper duds, and you even can speak the language, but now you must make the next major decision. When you enter a snowboard rental shop whether at your hometown or the resort, the question will be the same: "Do you want to ride regular or goofy?"

This refers to the orientation of your front foot on the snowboard. The right foot forward is referred to as *goofy*, a term from surfing; left foot forward is called *regular* due to the fact that most people are left oriented. Burton suggests that shops set up boards anticipating a ratio of 65 to 35, regular to goofy footed. It is a somewhat crucial choice but often overstated. Once you have started riding with one position, even if it is wrong, it's usually best not to switch. You will just learn to adjust to the error, and you will definitely have an advantage when it comes to riding switch.

Here is what this is all about. Unlike the frontal position when skiing, snowboarders employ a sideways stance which is determined by **putting the weight bearing leg foremost** on the board. The problem arises in determining which foot takes that front position. This has absolutely nothing to do with being right or left handed. Remember that.

If you have skateboarded or surfed, you will assume that same stance on the snowboard. If you have a weak leg or one which has suffered previous injury, you do **not** want it in the forward binding. Snowboard pros have various techniques for determining the frontal leg, most of them totally unscientific. Some use an eyesight dominance test which I have never understood. Others like to sneak up upon the unsuspecting person with a strong push, watching to see which leg goes forward first, thus interpreting it as the stronger one. Another popular method of determining which leg goes in front involves simulating sliding across a slippery floor. The forward sliding foot is the forward snowboarding foot. I find all of the above to be less than accurate.

Perhaps the best test is simply to ask yourself which foot you would use to kick a ball, remember that in such a situation, your body weight is balanced on the **non** kicking foot. Therefore **that stationary foot, not the kicking foot**, is your choice for frontal position. There is another test you could try, since you know of this in advance as you read these lines in the comfort of your home. Be conscious of your body as you stand around talking on the telephone or standing and conversing with people at work. Which leg do you seem to favor with most of your weight? That is your forward foot.

Ultimately, if you are still unsure, go with left foot forward. The very fact that this position is called "regular" should direct the undecided to accept that determination for their own initial riding experience. Remember that **it has absolutely nothing to do with being right or left handed.** Once you have decided your body orientation, do not belabor the point. Do not agonize over your decision. Stick with your choice and do not doubt it. Do not let anyone talk you out of it!

QUESTION:

WHAT IS THE DIFFERENCE BETWEEN A SNOWBOARDER AND A CERTIFICATE OF DEPOSIT?

ANSWER:

A CERTIFICATE OF DEPOSIT MATURES AND EARNS MONEY.

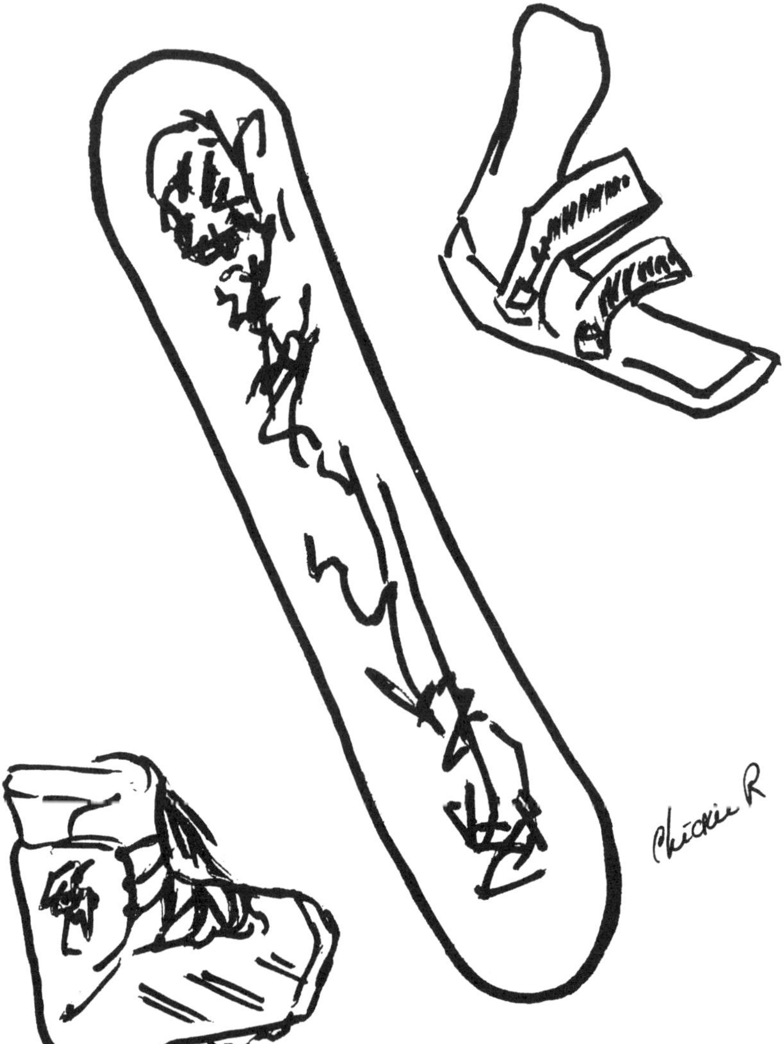
Chickie R

CHAPTER 6
THE THREE B'S
BOARDS, BOOTS, AND BINDINGS

Entering a snowboard rental shop can be a harrowing experience if you are not prepared in terms of the various choices you will have to make. Note that the focus of this chapter is on rental selection to guide you through that first initial equipment set up, rather than being a buyer's guide. For advice on purchasing, Chapter 13 has the in-depth approach on equipment which will make you a wise consumer. If you are planning on going that route, be sure to read this earlier chapter carefully as a preface to the more technical analysis which will come later.

Where to Rent

A decision must be made in terms of where to rent your equipment. Certainly, it is easier to rent at your local neighborhood where you have the advantage of time and place, as opposed to at the resort rental shop with the crowds lined up all rushing to make the lesson on time. However, the main advantage of renting at the ski/snowboard resort facility (and this is a very definite advantage) is the flexibility of the situation. If you have a problem such as a strap breaking (which often happens as a result of frigid temperatures), if the board is the wrong size, if there is a problem with the binding, *etc.*, all you need do is go to rental and get an exchange. If the equipment is from an outside source, you are stuck with it.

Another reason to rent at the resort mountain shop is because most ski areas offer special price breaks for lift, lesson and equipment packages. Those savings can actually be quite major. Beware, however, that if you plan on doing a resort rental, allow ample time to do so and go early. It seems as if there are never enough boards for all the people who arrive determined to take up the sport of snowboarding. Your second choice for rental would, of course, be the snowboard area local shops. Not quite as convenient in case a problem arises, it is nevertheless a lot closer than your neighborhood shop back home.

Boots

There are soft boots, and there are hard boots. Although skiers are somewhat naturally inclined to prefer the hard version because of their familiarity with a hard shell boot, that choice of boot also bears similarity to ski boots in its level of discomfort and lack of warmth. Don't even think about using your ski boots for snowboarding. Their flex pattern is all wrong for boarding, and they won't fit properly into the binding. Then, who should use hard boots? Hard boot systems are on the market for riders who want to race. This is life in the fast lane and certainly not the equipment suitable for a first time beginner. People often insist on going the hard boot route, but it is has been obvious to me over years of instructing that **it is very difficult to learn snowboarding in hard boots.** Do not create a handicap for yourself before you even go out onto the snow.

Soft boots offer the advantages of comfort, warmth, and ease of walking. Their design has been created for general riding which is referred to in boot sales marketing as *all mountain* and also for what is called *freestyle* which is for doing tricks and use in a snowboard park or half pipe. Try them on and select what is comfortable for you, the same as you would for any other sport shoe (keeping in mind the advice on page 41 regarding socks). Boots should be snug enough to prevent excessive heel lift but large enough that your toes lie relaxed on the footbed.

When you are sitting down putting on the boots it is okay if your toes seem to brush the front of the boot lining because usually when you stand up and bend your knees the lining will then stretch and your heel and toes will move back. If one size does not fit, dependent upon the rental shop's inventory, you can often ask for the same size but a different manufacturer. Also, you may have a choice of *step-ins* which refers to a boot specifically partnered with its binding arrangement, although this will create other concerns (see section on bindings).

You have been told to only wear one sock layer, and it should be a sturdy sport sock. A problem you will encounter is that your long underwear will come down into the boot area, causing bulk and chaffing. What you must do is pull the bottom edge of the underwear cuff up onto the calf area of your leg with flattened folds. If you have planned ahead, you will have done this before coming to the rental shop and might even have cut the underwear to shorten its length. If not, then it is something else to deal with as you try on boots. The only thing to enter the boot should be your foot and its single layer sock covering.

While on the subject of boots, it is important to remember that feet perspire, and your boots will be quite damp by the end of the day. If you are planning to wear them again tomorrow, be sure that you store them overnight in a warm place (not left in the car trunk). Open them up to insure air circulation and even consider using a hair dryer set on low to carefully enhance drying . I say "carefully," because it is easy to either overheat the boot interior or cause a problem with the hair dryer itself. There are many excellent products sold at ski shops which are specifically designed to dry ski or snowboard boots. If you are considering making such a purchase, you should select boot dryers which are portable as they will become an additional item on your snowboard trip packing list.

Boards

Snowboards are measured in centimeter lengths and the rental shop will guide you in the selection of the appropriate size dependent upon your height, weight, and ability level. There are boards designed specifically for men (wider in the board waist to avoid foot drag), but don't anticipate that these will be available in the rental inventory, although it should definitely be a factor for your consideration when it comes to making an equipment purchase.

Some resort snowboard schools are using special boards (not available for the public purchasing market) which have been designed specifically for teaching beginners. They are less rigid, having softer flex, and, to aid in the teaching process, edges are beveled to help avoid the sudden sharp losses of balance so upsetting to the novice (the dreaded snowboarder's slam). You can ask the rental shop if this is an option available to you.

Be sure to cite your experience level whether going out for the first time as a "never-ever" or having had some limited previous experience. The length and even style choice of your snowboard is predicated upon ability level and where you will be riding (race course, park, pipe, or all mountain). Height and weight are additional factors. *Snowboarder Magazine* uses a formula of multiplying your height (in inches) times 2.54 and then multiplied times 0.9 to determine board length in cm's (inches x 2.54 x 0.9). Rather than bringing along a calculator, you can usually place confidence in the rental shop to supply you with the proper board. Trust them; that's their business.

Since you are reading this book, and thus far on Chapter 6 rather than Chapter 13, then you are too much of a novice to consider the alpine racing board at this stage of your snowboarding experience, so there will not be a discussion of the subject here. Anyway, you should have been convinced that hard boots are not the best starting set up for a beginner.

The all mountain, also called freeriding boards can work fine doing park and pipe, but usually spend most of their time on ordinary mountain trails. These are the boards best suited for your first time out, and resort rental shops have a wide inventory to assure a proper match for your needs, provided that you make arrangements in enough time before their resources are depleted. Go early for the least hassle and the best selection.

Bindings

Hard boots require *plate* bindings. Be careful not to catch your fingers under the clamps, but hopefully I have discouraged you in this equipment choice when you are just starting out.

There are two options for soft boot bindings. The first entails a setup with two straps. There used to be offered a three strap system which gave more support with one strap across the upper foot, one over the instep area, and a third over the toes. That design has been pretty much phased out because three straps are one too many to deal with each time you step in or out of the binding, hence the more popular and practical two strap binding. These usually ratchet, are easy to work, and only have the disadvantage of requiring a deep exercise bend each time buckling or unbuckling is necessary. Negatives of strap systems are that because strap material is of a hard plastic, it can snap and break off from exposure to extremely cold temperatures. A second potential problem is that the strap itself may not reach far enough over the bulk of your boot to close the buckle. This is usually easily correctable in the shop where the technician can adjust the existing strap length, substitute a longer piece, or use a strap extender.

On the other hand, because you stand to attach, the alternate choice of a step-in system frees you from crouching down to buckle. It also eliminates the clumsiness of working buckles with mittened hands and will allow you to be first in the group ready and set to go. A complication is that this necessitates a companion boot to the specific system. For example, Clicker systems only work with their K-2 boots, Burton bindings require a Burton step-in boot, *etc.* This means that your choice must be predicated upon a comfortable fit of the required boot. As to the step-in binding itself, nothing is trouble free. Ice tends to adhere and harden around the metal plate and particularly the connection areas. Soft snow settles into clumps and must be pushed out, at times making it difficult to make proper contact.

A reason I do not recommend step-ins for beginners is although it is easy to place your front foot into the binding to ride a lift, usually you are doing this from the ski area base where it is flat. When you get off the lift and want to put your back foot into the binding, you must stand balanced on the board and negotiate back foot entry. This can be very tricky in a place with even the slightest pitch of a slope. Because you cannot enter the binding sitting down, that aspect becomes both a positive and also a negative thing. The only way to accomplish entry is to face uphill and, with your heel side, create a ridge of snow under the downhill edge as a stable platform to prevent sliding. It's tricky.

When step-ins were first introduced, they were extremely popular, but even for experienced riders the negatives of required boot partnering plus ice and snow build-up have lessened their popularity. Many freestylers have also returned to the buckle set up, feeling that it is a more stable and responsive binding. The binding is the communication transfer zone between your foot in its boot and the snowboard, so do not underestimate the importance of this piece of equipment.

Important: note that there is a shield like plastic piece, some eight inches or so high which protrudes perpendicular to the rear of the binding. This is called a *highback.* Some step-in systems have placed the highbacks inside of their boots which means that the boot has a stiff backing from the heel upward, making it very uncomfortable for walking. The better choice is to select a step-in where the highback is external as part of the binding system, located on the board rather than inside the boot.

How to decide between the convenience of a step-in versus straps? I have been using step-ins for many years so I am used to the inconveniences. As an instructor, I am constantly on and off my board so the advantages of speedy entry and, for me, more particularly that of quick disengagement, are obvious in terms of my needs. On the other hand, for the beginning snowboarder it is a decision weighing the advantage of a quick-to-ready position as opposed to the definite problem which exists in terms of understanding how to balance when out on the mountain slope with the forward foot already locked in. It is definitely a challenge not to fall over while placing the back foot into its binding or struggling to clear clogged up snow from the mechanism. The maneuver can be very frustrating.

Most shops only offer the buckle system for rentals, so you probably won't even have a choice. You can make a decision which is best for you later on when you are more experienced and deciding on purchasing your own gear. The bottom line, really, is that you must select the boot which fits you the best and go from there.

Binding Settings

There are several binding adjustments, all of which are referred to as *stance* and these should be checked out before embarking on your great adventure. Modifications are important as the previous renter most likely would have been a person with a very different body structure from yours.

1. The shop technician can either move the bindings closer together or farther apart. Stand on the board and be sure that your feet are a comfortable (stable) distance apart. According to the manufacturing companies, technically, stance should be equal to the measurement of distance from the ground to the back of the knee. Not in the habit of carrying a tape measure, I have focused on a totally different body measure. Instead, you can approximate the shoulder to

shoulder width distance and use that measure for how far apart your feet should be. In fact, I just measured my own body, and the knee-floor number is pretty much the same as my shoulder to shoulder measurement, so I guess that is why the system of shoulder approximation works just fine.

2. The technician can also make a second area of adjustment which involves stance angle. There is a disk which shows degree of foot direction slant usually marked in 3 degree intervals, with zero being straight across the middle of the board, equator like. The higher the angle number, the more the foot is tilted toward the front of the board, therefore the more suitable for advanced or more aggressive riders. Thus, for never-ever snowboarders, I suggest a stance for beginners of anywhere from 15 to 24 degrees for the front foot, and at least 9 degrees less for the back foot. For example, try 21° for the front foot and 12° for the back, or set at 15° for the front foot with 6° for the back foot. Determine which appears to be more comfortable when the knees are gently bent. Often boards are seen with that back foot set to zero which puts a great deal of unpleasant pressure and subsequent discomfort on rear leg muscles. Another problem with the back foot set to zero is that it becomes very difficult to bend both knees at the same time. Unfortunately, boards tend to exit rental at that setting.

Lately, for no apparent reason, I've been having people come for lessons with their feet set in what we call *duck foot.* The front foot points frontward in typical degree angle, but the back foot has been set with a negative degree angle, pointing in the opposite direction. This is a really functional set up for those doing free style spins and tricks, because the rider wants to be comfortable going in both directions, forward or backward (*riding switch*). The disadvantage for someone new to snowboarding is that with heels pointing inward and toes outward, it is very difficult to assume a flexed knee stance. When learning, you need all the help you can get, and hindering yourself with awkward binding angles is a definite handicap.

3. Bindings can also be moved for placement towards the front or rear of the board. If you are in the east, I am sure they will have been set slightly back of the center, but if out west and on a heavy powder day, it is preferable to be much more to the rear. Presumably, the shop will have anticipated that, but it's good to mention as it not only shows that you are knowledgeable but that you care.

4. Bindings are also adjustable in terms of the board width. It is very important for you to check to be sure that your heels or toes do not extend over the width (side edges) of the board edge. This is referred to as toe or heel drag which has the negative effect similar to if you are trying to go full sail on a boat while simultaneously dragging an anchor. The problem is common with men who have large boot sizes, and extra wide boards are available for such situations. This also is still another reason to use the freestyle soft boot set up rather than the hard boot as the latter is combined with a skinny race board thereby forcing the rider into a more angled (and aggressive) riding position in order to avoid boot drag.

Accessories

The board should have a *leash* and a *stomp pad.* The leash is a prehensile body part of the original snowboard binding design. In the early years of riding it acted as a safety strap to keep the board from soaring loose if the binding opened up, but today's bindings neither release without manipulation nor tear out of their drilled holes, yet the safety rules at mountains still require leash employment to the point that their lift operators will stop you if a leash is not present or attached.

The second item, the stomp pad, is important because it provides a skid proof surface for the back foot to rest upon when not buckled into the binding. This is either a mat or some sort of roughly textured device. Having a good stomp pad can make a serious difference in your ability to exit successfully from a chairlift. If either of these accessories are not on the board, be sure to request them.

Summary

In case you are feeling overloaded with information, here is a checklist of what you should do when selecting board, boots, and bindings:

* Say that you are a beginner.
* Be sure to state whether you are goofy or regular.
* Wear a sturdy sock without liner underneath.
* Ask for soft boots which should fit comfortably without the heel drastically slipping up. There may be a little play, but not more than about a half inch. Do not expect the form fit of a ski boot.
* Ask for an all-mountain board suitable for your size and weight.
* Check how far apart your feet are set and if your stance feels comfortable; know the binding angles and watch out for

toe drag.
* Be sure that there is a leash and stomp pad.

DO NOT LEAVE THE RENTAL SHOP WITHOUT BEING SURE OF THE FOLLOWING:

1. **YOU KNOW HOW TO WORK THE BINDINGS**
2. **YOUR BOOT FITS PROPERLY INTO THE BINDING PLATE**
3. **YOU CAN CLOSE THE BINDING STRAPS**
4. **YOU ARE SET WITH THE CORRECTLY DESIGNATED FORWARD FOOT**

Looking good is most of the game. To look like a pro as you leave the shop, you should carry the board under your arm, smooth surface inside next to your body, board nose (front tip end) pointing upward. Take care to wear gloves as the board edges can be very sharp. **You're now on your way!!!!**

QUESTION:

WHAT IS THE DIFFERENCE BETWEEN A SNOWBOARDER AND A VACUUM CLEANER?

ANSWER:

A VACUUM CLEANER HAS THE DIRT BAG ON THE INSIDE.

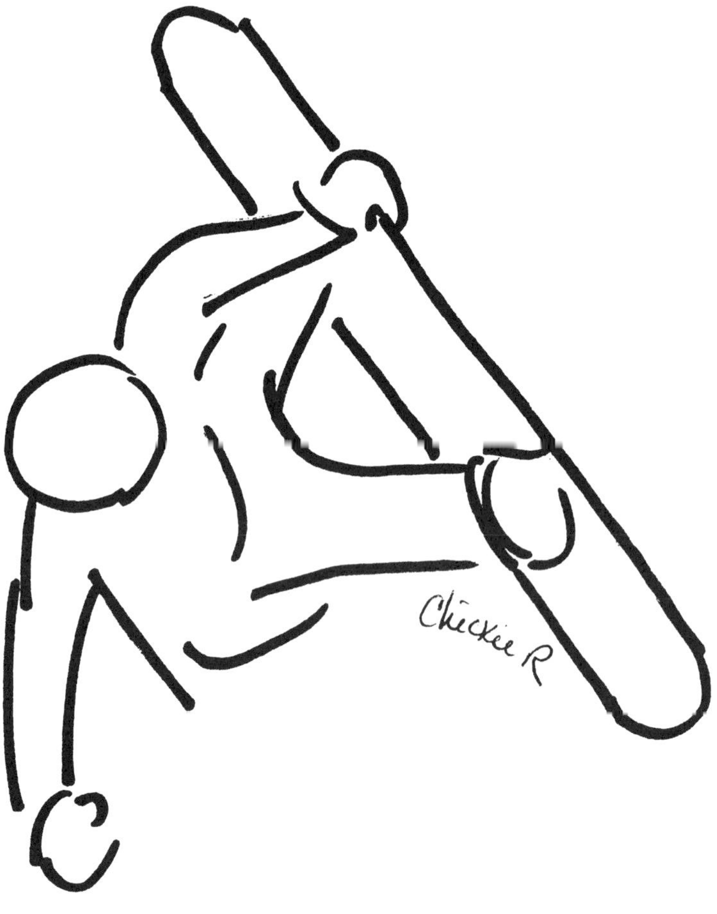
Chickie R

CHAPTER 7
AT LAST: HOW TO RIDE

You're ready to go for it. You are there, board in hand, with the mountain trail facing you, your lift ticket as an open invitation, **but wait**! Do not jump onto the nearest lift and think that you will figure out mastery of the snowboard on the way down! Even if you consider yourself one of those super athletes, snowboarding will not be a quick learn. You certainly won't look cool as you crash and burn, bashing your body while providing an entertaining view for the people around you and those watching from the lift. There's a way to learn how to snowboard and it's not by just "going for it." You can't muscle your way through this adventure.

Chapter 7 is absolutely not intended to be a substitute for an actual live, on the snow, in person, at the mountain, lesson. The better use of your reading is as a lesson introduction to advise on what to expect and even to help enact preparatory simulated movements which you can do in your home or hotel room environment, all in anticipation of your upcoming snowboard professionally coached lesson. By the way, notice that I have underscored "professionally coached." Friends can't teach friends how to snowboard. Knowing how to ride does not mean knowing how to teach riding. Professional snowboard instructors are not only experienced in what they do, but often receive additional training at their mountain plus maintaining active membership in a national organization, the American Association of Snowboard Instructors (AASI), whose membership requires attendance at instructional teaching clinics.

Upon going outdoors (and you can do this indoors if you are reading and simulating the experience), the first thing I have clinic participants do is to place the board face down on the snow surface. There is a optimal way to do everything. The correct way is to set down the board with its bindings on the snow. Beware; if resting with the base on snow, the board may suddenly take off sliding downhill, and you will be frantically chasing after it. Create good habits from the outset, and you will avoid inconvenience and embarrassment.

Since many snowboarder hopefuls have had an experience skiing, I ask people (with snowboards safely put aside) to assume the skier's posture. This means that one faces front, knees slightly bent, hands forward as if holding imaginary ski poles. Next, make your legs knock-kneed. Then, place a hand on the knee of the leg which has the (previously determined) forward position on the board . This is to remind you not to move that leg. Place the other leg behind and parallel so that you are now standing angled somewhat sideways, both knees slightly bent. You have now assumed a simulated stance position as if your feet would be locked into the snowboard bindings. Your head should be up and looking forward, although the trunk of your body has twisted somewhat sideways. Yes, it's a weird and awkward body position, and now you know why there are snowboard t-shirts sporting the word "twisted."

Now for the important part. As the kids say: "Listen up!" For beginners, here is **the Golden Rule of snowboarding: Weight on the front foot.** Later on, as you become more advanced, your weight will be shifted, but, for now, it is, I repeat, **weight on the front foot.** To be more precise, one really is placing *most* weight on the front foot. If you interpret the command as *all weight,* you would simply topple over!

Kinesthetics refers to awareness of your body and noticing how things feel. To create sensitivity and kinesthetic response to your stance, there are two important movements which I have people enact. Here you are, standing with both hands comfortably forward, and you are looking ahead. Be aware of the fact that your weight is placed on the front foot. Next, instead of continuing to look up and ahead, look down at your feet. Now-- where is your weight? Notice that your balance has shifted, and you are now standing with weight on your back foot. Try this several times, and, if with a friend doing it together, you will actually see the weight shift happening in conjunction with altered direction of view. Why is this important? **If you are snowboarding and look down at your feet or focus on the snow under your path of movement, your weight will have shifted from the front to the rear of the board** which, as will be shown, can have disastrous consequences. Test your body stance and the corresponding weight transfers until you are truly conscious of your body movements and their resultant effect upon balance.

A snowboard is designed to travel forward with your body weight pressuring towards the front end. That was one of the reasons it was so important to determine at the outset which would be your weight bearing forward foot. Therein is the crucial fact. If you weight the rear of the board, one of two things will happen. Either the board will react as if the rear is the front, spin around 180,° and send you downhill completely backwards, or, in a worse case scenario, the backward weight onto the tail of the board will cause you to resemble the silhouette of a speedboat with front end up in the air as you jet totally out of control with a horrendous forward lurch.

The lesson to be learned is actually rather simple. The ideal body position for the first time learner is to be comfortably balanced with weight dispersed approximately 70% front foot, 30% back, arms hanging at your side which means that the trailing arm is towards the back foot (remember that your stance is sideways, not frontal, on the board). However, if the situation should arise wherein you feel that you are losing balance, simply remember to increase weight on the front foot, and, for extra safety, lift your arms forward (as if holding a tray). Arms and shoulders are heavy; therefore, because you have brought that trailing arm forward in an emergency move, you have added stabilizing weight to the front of the board which will quickly reassert your balance. Do note that body position itself is always in flux, never frozen into a rigid stance; however, it is helpful to be aware of the optimal position for balance. It will come in handy.

Your general stance should be an athletic one with knees relaxed into a slightly bent position and ankles flexed. Get rid of that teeth clenched determined look which only reinforces your rigid body position. When muscles are held tense, they do not respond. Flexibility is what snowboarding is about. Anyway, aren't you out there to have fun?

You are, at long last, finally ready to buckle your front foot onto the board. Standing with the heel of your free (destined-to-be back) foot on snow bracing you, with the toe of that boot holding the board steady, place your other (front) foot into the binding and buckle up. Place the *front foot only* into its binding. Do the upper strap first, then the toe strap.

The newer systems simply require insertion and then ratcheting the strap to attain a snug fit (of course, you remembered to learn how to do all this while still in the rental shop). The boot should be firmly held in place to avoid shifting but not so tight as to cut off blood circulation. Next, connect the leash which either goes around the ankle or has a hook which snaps onto the boot lace.

Slightly lift up the board into the air, and feel how it is a clumsy weight. Put it back down, and tilt it to slide on the edges, toe side then heel side, in a sawing motion going back and forth, cutting lines into the snow (be careful if your practice session of these moves is on carpeting as your snowboard's edges can be extremely sharp and therefore cause flooring surface damage). If on snow, of course you should be standing on a relatively flat area where this will be safe to do. Place your free foot on the board, pressing close to, but in front of, the back binding. There should be that device called a stomp pad to mark this area with the purpose of giving this free foot a non skid surface. Stand balanced, pressing down on the toe side, lifting up the heel side.

Next, rock back onto your heels, this time lifting your toes upward. Do these moves numerous times to help create a type of muscle memory as this will become the motion used to *apply edge* and direct control when you are actually riding the board. Try to apply *torque* in twisting the board via ankle movements resulting in the front foot toes pushing down while the back foot toes move upwards, even though only the binding locked front foot is properly able to do its job. Such torsional movements help in tricky maneuvering across flat terrain.

Lift up your free foot and place it on the ground in front of the board. Then move it to the ground behind the board.

Now, being sure that you are on a level area where you will not slide, repeat these moves with eyes shut. All of these actions are to get you used to balancing. You are learning to maintain a balanced body position despite what the brain keeps perceiving as being relatively unstable.

I often begin my group clinics with these moves while indoors, out of the distractions of the mountain experience, so you should not feel foolish doing them off the slopes; however, at this point the indoor simulated (virtual) lesson must end. You are now ready for the real thing.

Skating

In a snowboard lesson the first actual movement skill involves familiarizing yourself with the feeling of locomotion on the board. Check the trail traffic of a relatively flat area, and, when clear, with only the front foot buckled in, try walking across (not down) the slope. Take very small sliding movements with the free foot on the uphill side and lined up pointing in the direction of travel. This foot will be in a normal body position whereas the foot in the binding is set in that awkward knock-kneed angle. Take tiny steps with the free foot and then slide forward with the board in this *skating* mode. Step...slide. Step...slide. Warning: if you look at your feet, the desired move will not happen. Look up and things go smoothly. It's that weight/balance thing again as looking down moves weight to the rear whereas looking up reasserts the forward balance and subsequently the forward motion.

For some reason this very important element of not looking down is extremely difficult for many people. You cannot ride a bicycle looking directly down at the pavement, you cannot drive a car focusing at the road surface, yet people seem mesmerized by the necessity of looking down watching the board travel on the snow. Apparently, it's a hard habit to break from the onset, but one which is extremely crucial to riding. Looking down at the snow is usually attributed to being nervous or extremely tentative. As the new rider gains in experience, he will lessen that downward glancing, but the problem is that looking down retards the very progress towards proficiency of riding ability. Anyway, if you don't look up, you have no idea where you are going!

Cross the trail, check for traffic, and return to the original site. Depending on whether you are regular or goofy, you will have to use the board's heel or toe edge to keep it from sliding away from under you as gravity along with the waxed bottom surface both do their job, and the board keeps trying to escape and go downhill. Try this simple exercise of *skating* a second time. You can even try putting the back foot onto the stomp pad and balancing as you glide forward. It is amazing to me how clumsy the first trip was and how much smoother it is by the second try. You are using new muscles and movement patterns, but you will find that your body will very quickly adjust. Be sure to look up and ahead, for the dual reasons of both balance and safety.

Unfortunately, it is exactly at this most frustrating point in the lesson when guests are struggling with the clumsy weight of the board slipping out from under them that the natural reaction is to be silently asking yourself, "Why on earth have I decided to take up this sport of snowboarding?" Do not listen to that inner voice! These first minutes are the absolutely worst part of the snowboarding experience. You must remind yourself to be patient as your muscles adjust to a different stance and movement pattern. Lighten up, and all of a sudden you will truly be enjoying yourself and having fun. I also think that these opening moments of the clinic sort of self-classify people and are self-selecting. There no wimpy snowboarders. It takes perseverance plus stubborn determination to learn to snowboard. I am always asked if snowboarding is difficult to learn. Yes, it is, at least for these opening moments. If you want a quick-to-learn sport that takes little or no effort, then this is not the arena for you.

The Straight Glide

Next comes orienting oneself downhill. Here, terrain selection is crucial. The location should be in a learning area with only the very slightest pitch. Many mountain guests make a serious mistake in that they assume just because a trail is marked with the green circle labeling it "easier" that it is suitable terrain for learning. This is where the expertise of your snowboard coach comes into play. He will know where to go away from distracting crowds and skier traffic and with a slope pitch gentle enough for a successful learning situation. Unfortunately, many resorts lack good teaching area which in itself often leads to discouraged first timers. Do not underestimate the factor of terrain. For the experienced rider, most slopes are not of major forethought in consideration. For the beginner, simply standing upright and moving several inches forward can be a challenge.

The *straight glide* involves placing the free back foot on the board either onto the designated stomp pad which is there to stabilize the unattached foot, or, if there is no pad, then try pushing your boot firmly against the back binding. Move forward into the fall line going downhill a very short distance and ultimately dragging the toe (not the heel) of the free foot, anchor-like, to create a stop. When demonstrating the straight glide I point out my tracks in the snow showing how far the dragged toe mark goes. This is in order to emphasize the fact that it takes a long time to actually come to a stop. Learning snowboarding, as in most skill sports, requires patience and understanding. Knowing that reactions take time for their effect, the track length before a halt helps the beginner to graphically see that the snowboard does not have power brakes. You will not have a sudden stop, although gradually the dragged toe will cause a ceasing of motion.

When instructing, I initially hold each person's board in place, checking out the body position to verify forward weight and eyes looking up. I ask each rider how he plans to stop, thereby confirming the fact that *he* is going to ride the board, not the board taking *him* for a ride.

As with the walking maneuver, the first attempt is usually a harrowing experience. The second try is easier. The third enactment is a sweet ride. Although the easiest movement to instruct, this straight glide is one of the important maneuvers. Whenever going onto or off any lift (poma, t-bar, or chairlift), the front foot is buckled in and the back foot free, and the rider must balance in this body position. To get off a chairlift, one must do this straight glide. While practicing, it is a good idea to be sensitive kinesthetically. Experiment with hand positions and remember that in case of emergency such as descending from a difficult steep chairlift landing, placing both hands forward as if holding that imaginary tray will provide you with the most stable balanced position. Mastering the straight glide is so very basic; maintaining balance in this situation will insure a confidence level now enabling you to learn turn enactment.

The Toeside Turn

Snowboarders do not refer to left or right turns. Rather, these are called *heelside* or *toeside* turns, due to the fact that direction depends upon the front foot orientation, whether regular or goofy. For the person who rides regular, a toeside turn brings them to the right, but it will be the opposite direction for the goofy rider. This is not a problem for the professional instructor who simply reverses the direction description and when necessary should be able to do demonstrations in both regular and goofy riding positions.

A turn is created by applying pressure on the board. If you have ever ridden a bicycle, you know that one must be in motion to create the turn. You can't jump onto the bike, quickly turn the front wheel, and expect to ride off at a sharply angled direction. Instead, the bike would shudder then fall over. It is similar on the snowboard. One must first be in motion before determining direction pressure. Therefore, start that straight glide. The very instant that you feel yourself moving forward, **gently begin to pressure downward onto the ball of the front foot.** This is an application of pressure to the toeside of the board which comes from a movement similar to what little kids call standing on "tippie-toes."

Note that it is a distinctly different move from pressing down with the toes themselves. That action would result in *edging* which could cause you to actually tip over, falling into the turn. Instead, focus kinesthetically on pushing downward at the area where your toes join the foot. You can exert some pressure from the back foot toes, but, because of the fact that the foot is not in the binding, it will have only a very slight effect. The board will slowly but gradually turn to the right. Nothing happens quickly. You saw how long it took to stop when toe dragging your free foot. The same slow reaction is true of the turn. The turn will occur but not suddenly, as it is a result of gradual mounting pressure on the board edge. Trust it to happen.

It is extremely important to look in the direction of travel. You can pressure your feet until the toes crush to the bottom of the boot, but if you are frozen into a gaze straight downhill, then you will go straight downhill! Look to where you wish to go. This bring us to the **second Golden Rule of snowboarding: Where you look is where you go.** Try this toe side turn with gradual ball-of-the-foot pressure and eyes focused on your destination to the right (for regulars) or left (goofy stance) doing it at least three times until feeling confident of the move. The key to determining success is to look back at your tracks. The edge of the snowboard should leave a clearly traced imprint of an arc cut into the snow.

The Heelside Turn

I have always found the word "heelside" to be problematic. The name of the turn is confusing. It really refers to the board's anatomy, not the rider's. The direction is oriented on the heel side of the board, but the turn is caused by pressure **on the rider's ankle area, not the heel**. A regular stance rider would exert pressure on the forward left side of his ankle on his leading left foot; goofy stance rider would pressure the forward right side of his ankle on his leading right foot. If instead, the rider rocks back onto his heels, the weight goes back (you don't want that!), and he will fall over backwards.

A disturbing aspect of the heelside turn is involved in creating the stop. One steps off with the free foot to enact that anchor-drag, but the movement is in the opposite direction of the turn due to the fact that you are standing oriented sideways on the snowboard. A regular stance person would have been heading left, but the stepping off foot abruptly pulls him to the right; goofy stance step off aborts the right oriented direction of travel with a sudden shift to the left. Beware. It is very easy to pull a muscle in the upper inside part of the thigh which will make you very unhappy. Therefore, the turn should be done very slowly and not ridden out a far distance, otherwise there is that inherent chance of picking up too much speed and the subsequent risk of muscle injury when trying to stop by stepping off the board.

The process of instruction is the same as that for the toeside turn. One begins with a controlled straight glide, then gently pressuring that forward part of the ankle and looking in the desired direction of travel. These factors will cause the desired turn which, for regulars, will go to the left and for the goofies, to the right. Practice makes perfect, and again, a trio of turns will give adequate experience.

My group clinics of about eight guests usually require a full hour to reach this level of instruction. It is always fascinating to see that by now these beginners will have mastered skating which initially was so challenging but now requires no thought or special effort at all. The straight glide is a confidence builder, and those who had found the toeside turn to be difficult usually have an easy time with the heelside, and the opposite is true for others. Ironically, the situation of preferred turn tends to reverse itself. Masters of the toeside suddenly become efficient at heelside, but at a loss of the former. It sort of comes and goes, but eventually all evens out, and you will enjoy going in both directions once two feet are firmly in the bindings which is exactly what comes next.

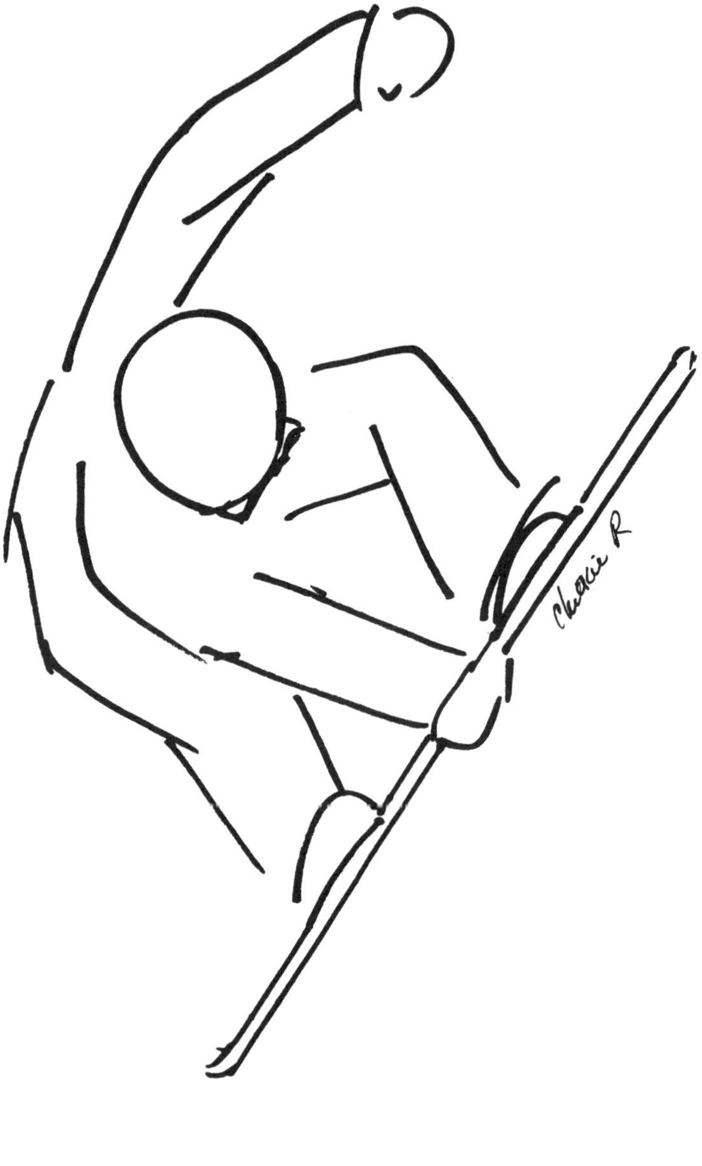

CHAPTER 8

THE MOMENT OF TRUTH: BOTH FEET BUCKLED IN

This is a reminder that the first six chapters of this book have focused on preparation for the snowboarding experience. From Chapter 7 forward, I have tried to anticipate and explain the typical lesson and movement skills to be mastered. As stated earlier, this is not a do-it-yourself guide. Instead, hopefully, after spending lesson time with a certified instructor, you will study these pages and further understand what you were attempting to accomplish out there on the hill.

The Responsibility Code

A good start is awareness of the Mountain Experience Responsibility Code. These rules are often posted at ski areas and are mentioned by instructors, but they are certainly important enough to be relevant and deserving of your full attention at this moment so here is the code:

1. Snowboard in control.
   This means that you must have the ability to stop or turn in order to avoid running into people or objects.
2. If you overtake another skier/snowboarder, you have the responsibility of avoiding them. If you are coming downhill, you must not run into the person ahead of you. This includes when doing jumps or coming suddenly onto a trail from in the woods.
3. Do not stop and block the trail.
   Unlike the skier who can stop and keep standing

without moving, when a snowboarder stops, he cannot balance and therefore must sit down. Be sure that you are sitting on the side of the trail and not blocking it or sitting out of view in a place where oncoming skiers and riders cannot see you.

4. Before traversing or entering a trail, look uphill and yield to those coming.
5. Observe closed trail signs and ropes.

   Closed trails are posted as such for your safety. Every season there are snowboarders who die when they fall into tree wells. The soft snow in the woods may look attractive, but it is easy to lose balance and be injured on ungroomed terrain where there are hidden stumps and other unseen debris close below the snow surface. A third reason to refrain from going under the ropes is because once in the woods, people usually cannot find their way back out. Ski patrol does not "sweep" these off limits areas, so you are on your own in terms of seeking rescue and at most areas lost persons are responsible for the cost of search party rescue operations.
6. You should have a safety strap (leash) on your board.

   Remember to hold onto your leash when first buckling in, as boards tend to take off rather quickly on their own when least expected.
7. Know how to use the lifts.

   If you are not familiar with how to ride a lift, ask the operator for help.

These rules appear to deal with etiquette, but they also relate to safety. If you ride out of control, you not only put yourself at risk but also endanger the safety of others. It's been such a long struggle over the years for snowboarding acceptance at ski areas, so it is incumbent upon us to be extra responsible and be good snowsport citizens.

Now that you know the rules, how do you actually *do* it?

The Moment of Truth

This is the moment you have planned for, outfitted for, traveled for, and read this book for! Remembering the fact that you are standing on a slippery surface, you do not want to take off downhill so be sure that you are standing with your board directed *across* the trail, rather than as if you were going to start riding straight down the slope. Sit down. You should be sitting on the snow, facing down the hill and now buckle in both feet. **Do not stand up!**

Although it seems unstable , with the back foot buckled in you will actually have much more ability to balance and properly control the board than before. Two feet buckled means twice the pressure power as before. The initial instructional stage of one foot off the board was not really a true sampling of what it is like to snowboard, because it only suggested a situation which is rarely enacted in terms of the time you spend on snow. Getting on or off a lift is momentary; the rest of the time you are on the board with both feet buckled in. If you are apprehensive about control, in a few minutes you will be learning new skills involving *edging (tilting*) and *twisting (applying torque to)* the snowboard. Trust the sequence of instruction. But first, there are a number of things to consider. To begin, for the best vantage starting point, the regular rider will be to the left side of the trail when facing down hill; the goofy should be on the opposite right side. This results in being toeside, the easiest way to start, when doing the initial *traverse* (movement across the trail).

The first thing is to understand is mobility. You are not like a turtle on its back. Instead, you have quite a range of movement. This is a good time to understand and accept the fact that snowboarders spend a lot of time sitting around on the snow, so you had might as well get used to it.

If you are a regular, stretch your right arm outward, lift your legs (with board attached), and roll over towards your right side onto your stomach. If you are goofy, stretch out your left arm to brace yourself as you roll over in that direction. You most likely will be wondering about the necessity of such gymnastics, but without learning how to roll over, you will be sort of "beached" upon the snow. You should now be facing uphill and on your knees. Without standing upright, you can shift-slide to the left or right. You can also do a frog leap forward up the hill. You will soon find yourself doing all of these moves at various times on the mountain.

Rolling over onto your knees to face uphill is a good habit to form because once you get onto steeper terrain you will find it relatively impossible to stand up facing downhill. I remember a conversation I once had with someone in the ski lodge cafeteria during lunch. He had spent the morning learning to snowboard, and, in response to my question of how he felt, he complained bitterly about his aching wrists. Of course, I made my usual little speech about never reaching out with your arm to break a fall as the pressure is simply too much for the wrist to absorb. "Oh, no," he said. "My wrists hurt from pushing myself up each time I fall." Thus, I learned of still another reason to roll over and get up facing uphill. However, the most important reason to do so is that facing uphill before resuming an upright position allows you to see oncoming skier/snowboarder traffic. Don't initiate riding until the coast is clear.

Edging

Ready to stand up? First, know that there is a movement called *edging*. Remember when you first put on the snowboard and leaned on its edges to make marks in the snow? Those edges of the board are sharp, and they are your brakes since you no longer have a free foot to drag in order to stop. As you slowly rise finding balance, use that uphill edge to hold you. Dig it into the snow. Too much edge, you will fall down onto your knees; too little, you will flop back downhill onto your head. Find the amount of edging which works for you.

At this point in a lesson, as the instructor, I am never more than several inches away and my hands are either holding onto the person or ready to do so (the bonus of taking a private lesson). Remember that practice of the toeside glide from the previous chapter where pressure on the ball of the foot causes the board to turn to the toeside direction (for the regular rider, this is a right turn)? You do not want to go straight down the hill; rather, the desired direction of travel is to go from the left side of the trail across the hill to the right side in a *traverse*. Now you will apply the newly added skill of edging. Toeside pressure and steadiness of vision will create direction; edging gives control. Keeping your eyes focused upon your destination across the trail, allow the board to slowly glide by releasing the edge just enough to let it move while gently asserting pressure on the ball of the foot. Be aware of maintaining most of your weight on that front foot. Be ready to tilt the board onto its edge if you feel the movement is too fast for your comfort zone. In an emergency, you can always drop to those padded knees.

Be assertive! Do not let that board take you for a ride! You have the ability to control all movement. Since vision is an element in this control, then use it wisely. If where you look is where you go, then why not look uphill? You can't ride uphill, so simply looking in that direction will naturally slow you down. Then, at the same time, press hard on that uphill edge of the board. Dig it in so hard that the board will cut the snow as you rock forward onto the toeside edge. Press down really hard with both feet to tilt the board. Those are your brakes!

The first time, like a new driver who slams on the brakes too hard, you will lurch toeside with a sudden stop. Reassert your balance. Now reapply pressure to resume movement across the hill. Keep testing those brakes gently, and you will quickly get the hang of it. Suddenly, sooner than you would ever expect, you will feel the thrill of actually riding the snowboard. This idea of looking uphill to slow down is taught here, the very first time you ride the board, and it also is a tactic discussed in a later chapter dealing with riding steeps. The point is that the better you learn these initial moves, the better rider you will become.

A note of safety in terms of your own self. You seldom learn to snowboard without ever falling. The trick is to understand and accept this fact and allow the fall to happen. Injuries occur (usually to the wrist or shoulder) when the rider reaches out to use an arm or hand to break a fall. As already stated, the wrist is a very small and vulnerable joint, especially if it is called upon to brace your entire body weight. When you think that you will lose balance, simply sit down. If you feel that you are falling forward, then drop to your knees.

Arms should be kept close to the body and never extended to prevent a fall. Falling does not have to mean being open to injury; it's just something which is part of the territory, although I truly believe that it is possible to give a no-falls lesson. Slow careful movements with patience in learning along with wise selection of terrain and good snow conditions are all important factors in a safe learning situation

It is important to avoid trying to muscle your way. Sudden violent movements cause sudden violent reactions. The reasons you tend to crash when learning to snowboard are usually because of weighting the back foot which causes loss of control, leaning on the downhill, not uphill, edge, which is why it is so important to keep reminding yourself if you are toeside or heelside so that you can concentrate on that edge, or lastly, when people think snowboarding is like sledding and try to go straight downhill. Then it becomes a matter of mere guts...how long they can maintain that upright position. Seek to avoid all of those scenarios.

Using specific skills of pressure, vision (where you look, whether across or up the hill) and tilting, you should traverse the trail. Then come to a total stop by jamming the toeside edge (for regular riders) super hard into the snow surface, and gently falling to your knees. Be sure to look back. It is important to see accomplishment. You can silently congratulate yourself on the distance you have traveled, all done with control of the board. Note the tracks you have left behind, and you will see where each time you forcefully edged to slow down and apply brakes to the speed of forward movement. Good job.

Ready to go the other way? Slowly stand, and, believe it or not, because this is much easier to do than it sounds, you will simply jump in the air and turn yourself around. That is, not all the way in a circle but just 90°, a quarter of the way, so that you will be in the same posture facing straight downhill as when with one foot loose we first were learning to do the straight glide. It helps to have a coach who steadies your board at this moment. You will now enact a heelside turn.

Looking across the hill, the heelside edge is now the *uphill* edge of the board (remember: it's catching that downhill edge which is disastrous). Some find this difficult because they tend to look straight down the hill and then lean forward with the pull of gravity onto the downhill edge, so it is important to focus on the direction of travel (which is across). It should be of some comfort to know that this heelside body position is actually the stronger posture compared to toeside. If you want to crush a soda or beer can, would you do it with your heel or your toe? Certainly, with the heel. This is because your heel side uses skeletal strength, whereas the toe uses muscle. Later on when doing a movement called *the falling leaf* you will dramatically feel the stronger position of heelside compared to toeside. At any rate, you should feel confident as you slow down (with edging) by rocking gently onto your heels and tilting the board, which acts as your method of braking as you slide forward and then edge again. Keep those toes (on the downhill edge) pushing upward inside the boot. It helps to mentally repeat the mantra: "heels down; toes up" as you do this traverse.

Move forward, then edge. Move forward, then edge. Control that board! With confidence of control you already should be having a good time out there. To stop, give an extra sharp jab with the heels down into the snow (skiers are usually good at this move as it is similar to the hockey stop), and then drop down into a sitting position. Look back at the trail to see your movement tracks and be proud of your accomplishment.

Each time you have finished going heelside you should come to a full stop; sit down and roll over. Continue practicing these traverses across the hill until you are really feeling in control of your moves. At first you may feel as if you are flying, but gradually you will get the knack for the proper amount of edging needed to control your speed. Note that your pattern of travel has been across, not down, the trail. For the beginner snowboarder, you do not want to go directly down what we call the *fall line* (akin to the path a snowball would take to roll down a hill), and if you have been used to skiing that "zipper line"remember that you are no longer facing downhill, but instead are sideways.

Although geometry has taught us that the shortest distance between two points is a straight line, the snowboarder disregards that mathematical axiom. The fun is in riding the board rather than reaching the final destination. Skiers are usually in a very big hurry to get to the bottom of a trail, whereas snowboarders may be meandering down, often stopping to ride a little snowbank on the sides. Their mind set is different from that of the skier, another reason why the sport is so much more appealing.

Linking Turns: As Easy As 1-2-3

It is usually when attempting to *link turns* (which means coming down the slope, turning without stopping) that people tend to experience what is called "the snowboarder's slam." Don't let it happen to you! There is a very simple way to avoid such a crash which is caused by catching the downhill edge. Using a 1-2-3 principle, know that there are three steps to linking a turn.

#1 You have done your traverse on, let us say, your toeside edge. Come almost, but not completely, to a stop.

#2 Looking downhill, steering with your feet, **allow the board to go completely flat.** This is a weird moment because the board wants to take off directly down the mountain. Count quickly, "1-2-3" which should actually take less than three seconds.

#3 Look across the slope and (leading with your ankle) ride onto the heelside of the board.

The reason people tend to crash while attempting to link turns is because the snowboard will not allow you to switch from one edge directly onto the other edge. **The board must have a middle sequence when it has no edging at all.** Think of it as akin to a shift car in that you must push in the clutch to change gears. You must go to neutral in order to change direction. Allowing the board to be flat, even for the slightest time, permits you to change edge pressure and direction of travel. It's really as easy as 1-2-3.

The Pivot

In case you didn't notice the phrase, I mentioned "steering with your feet" as the way to turn the board in the process of making a turn. What this really involves is moving the board into the desired direction of travel. Years ago, when the design of snowboards was much more primitive, instructors would teach people to reach out twisting the upper body and thrusting with their arms to create a turn. Nowadays snowboards are products of sophisticated engineering and such exaggerated upper body rotation is not only unnecessary in this situation but also undesirable. To turn the board with minimum effort and ride with ease, you simply move both legs to gradually pivot the board. This is what is meant by foot steering as it is an active movement of both feet to direct the board. Remember that snowboarding maneuvers occur because of crucial movements from the knee to the foot. That's the region where everything is happening.

The pivot is a movement around a fixed axis and you should learn from the outset that there is a difference in refinement of movement between the act of foot steering and that of enacting a pivot. The pivot is a more forceful rotation through the middle of the board. Pivots are crucial for sudden direction change particularly when doing moguls, but beginning riders who violently pivot all their turns are derisively called hitchkickers. Practice the pivot and also the more subtle foot steering. Both should be skills you have in your repertoire.

We all have a goal of looking good, and looking good is predicated upon a quiet upper body as the rider seems to glide effortlessly down the trail. We see skiers whose upper bodies heave side to side as they throw themselves into each turn. They still stay upright even though obviously they have no subtlety of movement. Such moves don't work as well in this sport. Snowboarders who think that mere physicality will do the trick, quickly learn that the more sudden and violent the move on the board, the more suddenly and violently one is heaved to the ground.

You should now go into the ski lodge to take a well deserved break.

Chickie R.

CHAPTER 9
TAKE A BREAK

Dehydration

Wanting to take a break is often a polite euphemism for stating the need to find time to go to bathroom. I know that this is a weird sounding suggestion, but be sure that you remember before flushing the toilet to look at the color of your urine. The brighter the yellow color, the more evidence you will have of your condition of dehydration.

Nowadays we tend to be quite aware of the need to drink plenty of water, but unfortunately, we tend to forget that hydration is important in the winter too. Snowboarding is a dynamic sport and, as you have seen, requires a great deal of body movement. With excessive body movement comes perspiration which, thanks to the wicking quality of your undergarments, will not have you feeling sweaty. Nevertheless, you need to replenish those lost body fluids. Also, if you have been out partying last night, chances are that you have arrived at the mountain rather dehydrated before you even buckled into your snowboard bindings.

The truth is that there is actually a greater danger from the effects of dehydration in the winter time than in summer, mostly because you would never suspect it. Dehydration leads to a situation where the body has difficulty regulating its own temperature, and this can actually result in hypothermia. To add to the problem, people often think that they are hungry when, in reality, they are thirsty. By the time you are thirsty, the body is already in serious need of fluids. So--while you are taking a break this is an optimum time to refuel the body with liquids. You have been concentrating hard and doing an athletic activity. Even if you don't feel thirsty or even sweaty, treat yourself to a good drink. But, of what?

To compound the problem of dehydration is the fact that the traditional beverage drink in a ski lodge is hot chocolate, which contains caffeine, a mild diuretic, thus only increasing rather than decreasing your state of dehydration. Sugar slows down the body's ability to absorb fluids, so you should also avoid soft drinks whose only true benefit is in their ice cubes. Coffee is certainly in the same category with hot chocolate in terms of its caffeine content. What's left? Decaf tea, decaf coffee, sport drinks, and good old-fashioned water. Not only will you feel more comfortable out there on the hill after a water break, but hydration leads to better mental concentration and physical coordination, plus, if in high altitude, it definitely tends to ward off altitude sickness symptoms.

Most of the major resort lodges have substantial space allotted to bars, but that doesn't mean alcohol is the beverage of choice for the break time. We all are aware of the effects of alcohol not only in terms of reaction time, but also ability to think clearly using good judgement. Snowboarding is challenging enough when totally sober; to go out onto the mountain after having beer or hard liquor can be absolutely disastrous. Save your partying beverage for *apres ski* time. And, by the same token, obviously, "recreational" drugs do not belong in the recreational activity of snowboarding.

Frostbite

Guys are not always so interested in facial skin care, but face cream is important to help avoid frostbite which finds its victims regardless of their sex. Frostbite occurs when the skin literally freezes. This is a real hazard on very cold days with low temperatures, exacerbated with wind (the wind chill factor). The best defense against frostbite is covering exposed skin with a neck gaiter or face mask along with a generous application of a frost guard cream such as those listed back in Chapter 3.

What does frostbite look like? Do you know the fuzzy white frost which develops on the outside and often inside of an ice cream container stored in your home freezer? That's just what it looks like on a person's skin. A patch forms, often ranging from the size of a dime to that of a quarter, where the skin first turns very white and then frost will appear. Treatment is simple. Watch for the appearance of a white area and then, *without rubbing*, place a non-mittened finger on the spot. The warmth of skin against the skin of the frostbite area will do the trick. Then, go indoors, out of the cold.

Remember that metal conducts temperature. Applying that principle, if you are wearing nose rings or other such facial body piercings, it means that the metal will make those areas more susceptible to frostbite. I watch my students' complexions closely, particularly those with such abovementioned body piercing, and I request that they do the same for me.

You can also succumb to frostbite in unexposed areas such as feet. The obvious signal is numbness and inability to move toes. The best safeguard is to simply accept the fact that you are cold and elect to go inside. But people, particularly in a group situation, and especially guys (that machismo thing again), do not like to be the first to say that they are cold. When one person meekly suggests that he is freezing, only then do others in the group tend to agree to take a break, often with a confidential whisper that they are also totally chilled.

Hypothermia

Hypothermia occurs when a person becomes so very cold that body temperature drops. Symptoms are fatigue, difficulty concentrating, lack of coordination, and most noticeably, shivering. It's easy to be aware of this danger when there are sub-zero conditions, but people can succumb to hypothermia in more moderate temperatures such as when it is misting or raining. Dampness takes away body heat, particularly when accompanied by windy conditions. Thus, unexpected cases of hypothermia can occur in weather temperatures which range from 32 to even as high as 50 degrees, given the situation of rapid body heat loss due to wind and rain. To safeguard: just be sure that you are dressed a little bit warmer than you would be normally in situations when you anticipate prolonged exposure to dampness.

With so many hazards, why get involved at all in this crazy sport?

On the contrary, it is simply more proof that snowboarding is so much fun that we do it in spite of the negative situations and risks involved. Why else would you drive for hours in bad weather on snowy roads, pay resort prices for hotel accommodations, worry about strategically dressing for varying temperatures, and go through complicated arrangements for equipment and instruction? It's a sport which will pay you back many times over in pleasure for the inconvenience involved and energy expended.

Chickie R

CHAPTER 10

REVERSE GRAVITY: WHAT COMES DOWN MUST FIRST GO UP

Before you even think about *how* to ride a lift, first decide *where* you want to go. That may sound obvious, but so many times people wind up on the wrong trails simply because of failure to study the resort map. When finishing a clinic, ask your instructor for advice on what trails would be appropriate for your ability level. The green circle emblem designates easier trails, the blue square marks more difficult trails, the black diamond is for most difficult, and the orange lozenge announces the terrain park. The problem is that there are no plus or minus signs within the three trail marking categories which means that some of these may be relatively easy for their labeling, while others are much more challenging.

Although a trail is marked green (easier) it does not necessarily mean that it is the place for you to begin. "Easier" is a comparative term, that is, in relation to the rest of the trails. What you want is not "easier" but "easiest! " Major resorts have set aside learning areas for first timers. That is where you want to have begun. Once you have mastered the basics of boarding there, be sure to ask the best place to venture next. Terrain selection happens to be one of the most important factors in having a successful snowboarding experience.

Snow conditions are also a major element. Ice can make that easier green trail into a black most difficult one.

Conversely, fresh powder is what we call "ego snow" because it slows everything down and is forgiving of your mistakes and can make difficult trails into a sweet pleasure ride. Even the time of day has an influence, not only because of the weather's impact upon snow in terms of softening up or freezing hard, but because as the day goes on, the trail surface may become slick and slippery due to an appreciable depth of snow which has become scraped off from skier traffic. That smoothly groomed trail of 9:00 a.m. may be a serious mogul (bump) field by 3:00 p.m. Ask around before selecting a lift; choose your destination wisely. It may seem carefree to randomly go where the closest lift takes you, but you might not be so happy once faced with the prospect of coming down the trails serviced by that lift.

Be sure to have a trail map and study it carefully. In selecting one lift over another you may eventually find yourself very distant from your starting point, even so many miles away that you will be required to take a bus to return to your starting place. You came there to snowboard, not to ride public transportation.

Regarding chairlifts, generally speaking, most women tend to be rather terrified at the prospect of riding a chairlift, much less with a snowboard awkwardly dangling from their feet. Men may also feel the same way, but seldom voice their concern, although that doesn't mean they don't share such reluctance. One gets over this inhibition when faced with the prospect of hiking or mastering one of the non-airborne types of lifts which pull you uphill as you must balance on the snow. We know that according to the laws of physics, what goes up must come down. As a snowboarder, however, I am more concerned with the fact that to go down, one must go up.

For all lifts, except gondolas and trams where you carry your equipment inside, your front foot is buckled in, and the back foot is free. Now is the time to review your skating technique and the straight glide, both of which were the first maneuvers you did when learning to snowboard. This is especially important if it is the first you are out for the season or if time has elapsed since you have been riding. Go to an area which is not congested and review those motions of walking and sliding the board forward with the free back foot on the stomp pad. Then you will be ready to enter the lift maze.

The easiest of the surface lifts, or "drags" as they are called in Europe, is the *poma*, a disc suspended on a spring. I prefer to ride the poma with the disk under my right arm (under the left arm for goofy riders), tucked up tight above the elbow towards the armpit so it will not pop out. Balance with free foot on the stomp pad, leaning back slightly to compensate for the initial forward jolt and ready to then transfer weight onto the front foot. Hold the post with both hands, look ahead at the tracks, and enjoy the ride. Getting off is easy. Just let the disc slip out, and it will pull up out of your way.

If the poma runs for a very long distance, as is the case in some European ski areas, then it is better to place the disc between your legs. Do not sit down, and do not let it pop out. Of course, such advice is easier said than done. Skiers place the poma disc in this position between their legs, but it is easier for them as they face frontward, not in the snowboarder's sideways stance. The worst poma I ever went on was in Italy. The lift traveled up along a ridge with a horrendous drop on one side. Fear of falling off was what made me stay on! Another unforgettable poma was in Chile where, after a long steep haul, it then made a 90 degree turn and continued onward and upward. In comparison, pomas in the United States are quite user friendly.

On the other hand, the worst *t-bar* I ever went on was at that same Chilean resort, mostly because it just seemed endless. The t-bar is a hook shaped wooden bar which is placed behind your butt, as if it were a seat, but you must not sit on it. The trick is to balance enough on the bar as it pulls you uphill without allowing it to slip out from under you. As with the poma, you look at the path, balance on the front foot, and really focus on maintaining this precarious position. The good news for both of these lift systems is that if you do fall off, usually there is no fearful drop because you were on the ground surface all the time.

Compared to the prospect of managing to balance on these surface lifts, even a person who is unhappy with heights realizes that the chair lift is starting to look like an appealing alternative. In fact, once you have succeeded in getting onto the chair seat, it's rather comfy. As with riding other lifts, the front foot is buckled in; the back foot is out. For your very first attempt it is best to ride on the chair with someone experienced, but not on a full chair. In other words, if it is a "quad" which seats four, request to ride as a threesome. This will give you more maneuverability room when getting off at the top.

Move up to where there is usually a marked line for the loading zone, look over your shoulder to see the chair coming towards you, sit when you feel it bump the back of your legs, pull down the safety bar (warning your lift companions so that their hands or heads are not at risk), and enjoy the ride. If you are not particularly comfortable with the height, simply do not look down. For those who find the weight of a dangling board uncomfortable, one can balance the board somewhat horizontally over the toe box area of your free foot which then acts as a support under it.

While riding the chair is a good time to watch and study other riders beneath you. Do some mental coaching in observing their strong moves which will help in creating an image of how you will be handling the same trail. Some useful "do nots" for the chair ride: do not fuss with your hat because you may drop it; do not ever take off a glove because you will be *sure* to drop it! Instead, talk to your lift companions but pay attention to the length of the ride in order to raise the bar in time and be ready to unload.

I advise my students on a foolproof way to dechair. First, while on the lift but nearing the end, plan ahead by placing your free foot on the stomp pad. Look down at this placement. Relax and feel free to move that foot away. You will NOT glance there again, but, trust me, you will remember without looking down upon landing where to put your back foot onto the board. As you approach the landing area the chair may slow down if it is a "detachable." A sign will tell you to lift the safety bar. Steady yourself with hands on the edge of the chair seat, although it is not necessary to inch forward. Now, as you approach the unloading area, be ready to stand, weight on the front foot, free foot on that stomp pad, looking ahead to where you want to go.

The secret ingredient is that you should hold both arms straight out in front of you while looking up, not down. Direct your vision forward using your arms as a sight line. Don't be concerned about looking down. Because you had simulated the move, your back foot will find its place on the stomp pad. Note that if, instead, the free foot is set onto the snow, you will spin around it (similar to the way the fixed point of a draftsman's compass needle causes the pencil to circle) with disastrous results in that not only do you lose your balance, but you will also knock over your chair traveling companions. You have a stomp pad; make use of it.

The outreaching arm position will bring your weight forward and initiate the motion needed to glide off. You may look silly with this arms out position, but you will look sillier if you do not do that and instead look downwards or place your free foot on snow, both guaranteed to make you crash land!

You will soon realize that the biggest problem in getting off the chairlift concerns the skiers who are stopped in the unloading zone. They carry their poles in hand for the chair ride and now are busy affixing the strap handles over bulky mittens or gloves, totally unaware that they are blocking the chair exit area and of your inability to avoid the place where they are congregating. Mountain courtesy and safety both encourage you to yell ahead: "Excuse me, please clear the way!" It is a much better strategy than smashing into them.

Be sure to move quickly away from the path of the chairlift. You will now have to sit down, buckle up, and orient yourself as to your destination.

QUESTION:

WHAT'S A KNUCKLE DRAGGER AND WHY WOULD YOU WANT TO KNOW?

ANSWER:

YOU!

GET USED TO THE TERM BECAUSE THAT'S WHAT EVERYONE WILL NOW BE CALLING YOU

Chickee R

CHAPTER 11
IS THAT ALL I NEED TO KNOW?

By now, you are rather proficient at doing both a heelside and toeside traverse (in non-snowboarding language: going either direction diagonally across the trail), and your ability to link turns is actually getting impressive. You feel ready to do it all.

Continuing Education

A problem is that at this point people tend to think that their instructional learning phase is done. Wrong. Although the resort area's special introduction to snowboarding program might have ended, it doesn't mean that you are *there* in terms of learning and accomplishment. Snowboarding consists of more than basic traverses on extremely moderate terrain.

On the other hand, this does not mean that you must take costly private lessons. Check the resort's marketing brochure for the clinic programs which are usually quite a bargain because the industry is geared to keeping people interested once they have become engaged in a snowsport. An advantage of the clinic is that friendships are formed within the group so that often you will have companions for riding when the clinic ends. If you can afford it, private lessons offer the luxury of instruction geared to your own rate of progress plus the potential for a continued relationship with one snowboarding pro as your coach.

Either way, it beats going out on your own trying to

remember what the instructor told you last week, or what you *think* you were told. Memory is deceptive with the added factor that differing snow conditions require different techniques.

The "You Can Do It" Syndrome

Beware of overconfidence and beware of friends who invite you to come along to ride difficult trails with them, reassuring you with the words, "You can do it." Human nature is such that once people have learned to do certain skills, they tend to forget or discount their own initial fears and difficulties. Your buddies have already forgotten what it was like for them as a beginner and easily underestimate the difficulty which confronts you. Your struggles should not become their source of entertainment.

You will survive, but at a cost in terms of doing a lot of falling down and generally bashing your body. Falling is a very negative thing. It is not only demoralizing, but it can cause injury. Yes, you learn with challenge, but being brought onto too difficult terrain and being discouraged is not exactly productive. Gaining mileage is key to improvement, but, as stated in the previous chapter, terrain selection is a critical element. Supervised moves with a qualified instructor are the way to go. It's a matter of quantity plus quality.

The Falling Leaf

Do not think that because of my background as an English professor, that the name and selection of the following exercise was my idea. *The falling leaf* is a standard maneuver in instructing snowboarding. However, because of my study of American literature, I always recall an E.E. Cummings poem of that same title when teaching the falling leaf. Although the poet's theme is the subject of loneliness, the letters inside his parentheses which spell out "a leaf falls" conjure up the solitary image of the back and forth swaying floating motion of a single leaf as it falls from the tree to the ground. That is exactly the movement pattern which you will do on a gentle slope. The poet's image may help you to understand what is involved here.

The poem reads as follows:

l(a

le
af
fa

ll

s)
one
l

iness

from *E.E.Cummings: Complete Poems 1904-1962,* edited by George J. Firmage, Liveright, New York, 1991, p. 673.

The falling leaf snowboard action is basically a pendulum-like movement to the right and to the left progressing downhill on the trail. Learning to do the maneuver will strengthen your riding skills and be a first introduction to the freestyle move of riding backward, called *switch.*

The action is easiest to begin learning to do from the heelside, your stronger body position. You are standing on the board, facing downhill. Remember that where you look causes direction, and weight on the front of the board creates the desired force. Now, turning your head to look over your left shoulder, employ the additional weight of both arms by swinging them over to the same side. You will move horizontally on a slight diagonal across the hill. Just go several feet, then rock back onto your heels (tilting the board to enact edging) to stop. Next, look the opposite way to the right. Swing your arms onto that direction, and weight your back foot, which will cause you to slide backwards. Yes, the back foot. Then tilt the board on edge again to stop. You will have gone in reverse horizontally, riding *switch*, on the diagonal, near where you started, but considerably lower down on the slope.

This is possibly the most important maneuver you will ever learn for survival on terrain which is too difficult for you to ride. Do the falling leaf, sliding from side to side, going forwards and then riding backwards, a number of times. Turn around and see how far downhill you have efficiently traveled. This is the technique to use when the slope is too steep, you are too intimidated to turn, and/or you are having a problem for whatever reason in coming down some portion of a trail. Once learned, it is easy to do, and it will literally save you. Practice on the toeside, but know that this will quickly become tiring because the calves of your legs will get quite a workout. Remember that toeside relies upon muscles, whereas heelside uses the body skeleton for pressure support. That is why the heelside falling leaf is a thing to practice until it has become an integral part of your riding repertoire.

Sideslipping

Sideslipping is another emergency technique to use when you want to get down an area of the trail without doing a traverse or trying to turn, although it is not as sophisticated a move as the falling leaf and, therefore, not really as effective. You simply tilt the board onto its uphill edge and allow it to slide slightly, controlling the speed of the gravity-pull acceleration with reassertion of the pressure tilt, *edging* as a way of applying the brakes. The maneuver works, but your body may feel like a jackhammer as you rumble over the surface for a prolonged period of time.

Riding Switch

You've already done this freestyle maneuver when you went backwards doing the falling leaf. That was simply going backwards in a traverse. Riding backwards with linked turns used to be called *going fakie,* but now is referred to in snowboard jargon as *riding switch.* This is a fun thing to do and is a requisite introduction to freestyle tricks. It's also handy when you are in a jam and don't have the room or maneuverability to go forward. Think of your intro lesson to riding: pressure on the front foot, looking in that direction. Just do the exact opposite: pressure on the back foot, twisting around your upper body to look in that backward direction. You are doing a reverse of the norm, having switched. What was the nose of the board is now, in effect, its tail. Concentrate on how you previously have made a forward turn with head and shoulders aligned. Do it in the reverse direction.

If it feels awkward, that is an expected reaction because your lower body will be twisted since your feet are set in an angle binding toward the nose of the board. You are now oriented towards the board tail. Those who do a lot of switch riding prefer to have a *duck foot* binding setting (each foot with heels together, toes pointing outward in opposite direction, ballet style) and use a free-style twin tip board which has the nose the same as the tail so it is design engineered for movement in either direction. To help you feel more balanced, try working your knees pointing inward when toeside and outward, cowboy style, when heelside, causing the board to flex torsionally. Do a switch traverse, allowing the board to seek the fall line, then be sure to lean downhill with bent flexed knees oriented as stated above, looking across to enter the new traverse and finish the turn. Be sure that your practice is done on a very flat learning area.

Garlands

As you must have observed, imagery is very important in snowboard coaching, and the garland is like the decorations which drape from branch to branch on a Christmas tree. You will trace similar loops on the snow in a modified traverse. Instead of going diagonally across the trail, go about one third of the way and then head uphill (look uphill and pressure the front foot). You can't ride uphill, so the board will stall out and then proceed to slide backwards. Allow it to do so for a few feet, sort of rocking backwards. Tilt the board on edge to stop, and then, reasserting your direction, go another third of the way across the hill, repeating the uphill motion. Rock back, then go to the final segment of the trail.

The good thing about doing garlands is that you get many chances to control the board as it traverses, rather than going all the way across the trail, cutting through downhill traffic, and then worrying about what will happen when you eventually reach the other side. Doing garlands is an excellent technique for confidence building because you are riding the board, not letting the board take you for a ride. Picture in your mind those Christmas tree garlands and go for it.

Looking Good with Shaped Turns

Looking good on the snowboard results from feeling at ease. The more confident you are, the better you will look. One way to help achieve rhythm is to understand turn shape. The goal is to make round turns. To pivot is to rotate about an axis. Although the pivot is really an important move, particularly when faced with uneven bumped up surfaces (these are called *moguls*), it is often a problem when novice riders indiscriminately pivot their turns. Pivoted turns spin around to change direction. They are quick which is why the rider employs them because the time facing the fall line is frightening, and we want it to be only for the briefest instant; however, the effect is jagged, and the resultant move is what I call windshield wiper turns.

With confidence comes trust in your ability to slow down and negotiate the turn with slow soft pressure and wide arcing moves. Think of the turn as having three distinct regions: the beginning, middle, and the end. The first phase is easy, but the middle finds you facing directly downhill in the fall line which is the danger part. It is here that you must calmly and gently direct the board using foot steering and a twist of pressure to create *torque*. Sorry for the technical terms, but pressure on the front with slightly lesser pressure done by the back foot on the opposite edge will cause the board to employ what is called *torsional flex*. It will help the board to glide smoothly through the turn.

I tell my students that it's all basically reduced to a Kierkegaardian leap of faith; you have to believe in it, and then it will happen. Too much back foot pressure causes abrupt turns, which we refer to as "hitch-kicking," so this will take some careful consideration to get the right refinement of timing and intensity of pressure. Rather than focusing on the physics involved, simply try to round out the turns into giant curved C shapes.

Actually, it's sort of fun to experiment with turn shapes in regard to the alphabet. Do some Z shaped turns to help define your goal of a C shaped turn. How about trying an S turn, or even a J turn? The former simply means that the turns are a C shape followed by a C done reversed, but the J is an exciting challenge as you go straight downhill then are "saved" by a rounded turn out of the fall line. Try J and reverse J turns (always reverting to easier terrain when experimenting with new moves), and you will really gain confidence in your turning ability. Skiers call these *fish hook turns* because at the end there is a backwards slide (similar to that which occurs when doing garlands).

By now you must realize that you are no longer in the beginner category, and you will have loosened up on the axiom of weight on the front foot. Back foot pressure is needed to do the falling leaf, the garlands, and the J turns. In truth, if we had x-ray eyes to see into the boot, we would notice that the crucial joint at work here is the ankle which flexes so that pressure moves are initiated from the toe or heel of the foot, and within those areas we can see that the pressure is moving from the big toe across the foot to the little toe, all during the turn sequence. Your back foot is starting to play a more active role. Relax, and your body will work out the best way for you to balance with sensitivity to adjust stance not only fore to aft on the board but also vertically by flexing the knees.

Another variation on the turn has to do with frequency. You can make big fat long turns which swallow up much of the trail. These are called *wide radius turns* and tend to be good practice as you have plenty of time to ride the edge of the board and concentrate on the roundness of the turn shape. Narrow trails call for *short radius turns*. These must be done quicker and take up less space as they are more within the fall line.

Imagine that the trail you are on is only of limited width and that you have no choice but to keep turning. How many turns in a row can you make? Another skill developing exercise is to try doing a spiral, starting with wide radius turns and then reducing their size until they are narrower and narrower. Next, do a reverse spiral, with turns getting larger and larger.

Look ahead to a specified point such as a tree alongside the trail or a lift tower, and see how many turns it will take for you to arrive at the destination. There is use for all size turns. It is a good idea to know that you can and should be varying your turns without compromising the desired round shape. One caution, however, is to make these balanced as we all have a tendency to favor one direction and thus hold the turn longer when going that way. Try counting to insure that you hold the toeside turn for the same number of beats as you devote to the heelside turn. Doing a repeated 1-2-3 turn sequence also forces you to turn in rhythm as opposed to turning as a way to avoid irregularities of the snow surface.

Fore/Aft Balancing and Upper Body Rotation

Where are you at the end of those turns? Are you leaning aft, what we call "in the back seat?" Remember the reason why you selected the stronger foot to the front position? If at the conclusion of the turn your weight has shifted to the back foot, then your next turn will not be so easy to initiate. On steep terrain, being back leads to a quick wipe-out. Many skiers try to muscle their way through turns with upper body rotation, resulting in sloppy moves. The snowboarder who does so will quickly tire as he has a heavier platform to throw, and with dire consequences. Upper body rotation is needed to do freestyle spins and deal with heavy snow, but in other situations it simply makes it more difficult to execute the next turn. Do not forget that one of the goals of a snowboarder is to look at ease and ride with flow. That doesn't happen to be the image with flailing arms and a heaving upper body.

More Turning Tricks

Another interesting thing to do with turns is experimenting with arm/hand position. Try making a turn with your hands in different positions: *i.e.* on top of your head, hanging down at your sides, raised in front as if holding a tray, clasped behind your back, akimbo at the hips, or straight out like airplane wings. You will quickly find out how your turns are initiated. The turn should be enacted with movement originating from the knee to the foot. The upper body should be quiet. If you are off balance on your turns, do these above mentioned hand position drills repeatedly to get rid of upper body movement (*rotation*), and instead you will learn to glide through with a balanced smoothness. I once spent an entire season working on riding with my hands behind my back, Hans Brinker style. It was fun and helped me to focus on my balancing along with eliminating wasted upper body motion.

The airplane wings image may be used in another drill which is also done instead by some snowboard instructors with the use of bamboo poles. When traversing the hill, your body should be perpendicular (remember your geometry) to the trail, which results with shoulders being parallel to the slope of the trail surface. In essence, because the hill slopes, you should also slope. In other words, your uphill shoulder should be higher than your downhill shoulder. When you turn to traverse to the opposite direction, the shoulder positioning should also be reversed. Try that airplane wing arm posture, and you will quickly see the obvious. Do it with a partner and report to each other on your observations. This is the same principle which runners use as they lean forward downward when running downhill instead of pulling back which is counterproductive. The lower downhill shoulder will help you create a smoother more balanced turn.

Bend Ze Knees, Five Dollars Pleeze

This phrase was always the classic ski instructors' joke. Learning to ski was simply reduced to a matter of bending the knees. Snowboarders must also bend their knees, but it is interesting to self experiment to fully understand the effect. Do a traverse across and back, riding the board as low as you can possibly go. Next, start low then suddenly stand very tall, as if someone were pulling you erect, caveman style, by the hair. How did it feel? Which way had you going faster? Which made you go slower? Staying low on the board exerts pressure which slows you down. The sudden rise results in what we call *unweighting* and the board will pick up speed. Do not take my word for it as it is important that you can feel the difference yourself. The bottom line is that you must have flexibility in the knees to adjust to the always changing snow surface. Knowing that going low to place pressure on the board which slows you down can be useful to enhance your braking moves.

Why is this important in the turn? The best explanation I have ever seen is in Chapter 37 of a book about skiing, *The Athletic Skier*, by Warren Witherell and David Evrard, published by The Athletic Skier Inc., Utah, 1993. Bikers are always aware of centrifical force as they bank around turns, and if you ever helped out removing laundry from a washing machine you would have observed that when the machine spins, the laundry flies away from the center and is pushed outward onto the sides of the tank.

Think of the turn as the letter C and notice that there is an inside and outside area. At the top of the turn, gravity is pulling you down the hill, but centrifugal force compensates for this by pressuring you in the opposite uphill direction (just like the laundry). In the middle of the turn, you are in the fall line, with gravity causing you to pick up speed. At the end of the turn, you have gravity pulling you downhill and also centrifugal force as both are now on the outside of the C.

The increased pressure of not one but two forces (gravity plus centrifugal) pulls you downward. That is why it is so hard to control the board at the end of the turn, to slow down, and to tilt on edge. Instead, the board *skids* leaving a banana peel track on the snow, rather than the sharp line we desire (as in a *carve*). Skidding diverts your forward motion by also going sideways. As such, it is an ineffective move.

Back to the subject of the knees. If you stand tall to

start the turn there will be increased acceleration in a controlled body position. By lowering the body, bending the knees at the final part of the turn, you can counter the effect of gravity plus centrifugal force, thus reasserting control at this last phase. You won't have to do a braking motion by tilting the board so much on edge; it is simply done by bending your knees which lowers your body mass and slows you down. That is, until you rise up to initiate the next turn.

One other aspect of the bent knee story is that rather than thinking of the rising/sinking action in terms of unweighting, you should also be using your knees to retract the board. In other words, the knees become something like shocks on a car (or a mountain bike). Stiff legged riders will be jolting their bodies each time they go over a rut, whereas those with flexible knees absorb these irregularities by drawing up the board.

I just bought a new car, and now I am fully aware of the fact that the shocks were in bad shape on my old car. Before, I pretty much felt each irregularity on the roadbed but now it's smooth going on the same route. As stated, your knees actually enact the same function as those shock absorbers on the car. Even with the best grooming, no ski trail is ever perfectly smooth. With flexed knees, you can absorb the uneven surface. When riding the chair lift, watch other snowboarders on the trails below. It's easy to pick out those who work their knees for a smooth ride. The stiff legged snowboarders tend to bend over at the waist with their rear ends sticking out. They certainly don't look good, and they also lack the ability to absorb the terrain.

So, as they say, "Bend ze knees, pleeze."

Skidding Versus Carving

I took ski lessons for many years and always was admonished for "skidding" my turns. I dutifully apologized, although I never really had any idea what that meant nor how to correct it! That's the problem with technical vocabulary which snowsport pros tend to use and of which the public has no understanding. As explained on page 142, there is a reason according to the rules of physics which causes skidding, but perhaps it is simpler to explain the goal of the carve. Imagine a deeply outlined letter C clearly delineated in the snow to show the path of your track through the turn. It's the difference between the skidded turn mark which looks like a banana peel laid out onto the snow compared to a sharp clear knife cut of a line. To accomplish this, the board must have been on a tilted edge all through, with a quick skip barely perceptible in the middle where you switched to the opposite edge. If smooth turns and speed are your goal, the means to that end is the carved turn.

Think of one of those big city fire engines with a driver in front and another steering the back end; the board is your fire engine and it needs to be guided. In the midpoint of the turn you must steer the board by applying pressure to the tail end, forcing it to accept, on a tilt, the same line of travel as the front edge has gone. Technically, this is described as employing torsional flex and thereby creating the carved turn. You need not know the vocabulary, but you should understand the objective.

By cutting a clean line in the snow there is less drag on the board as it progresses forwards without simultaneously splaying out sideways into the skid. This is a more practical move than the skid which is awkward and simply is a sort of inefficient way to make a turn. You might not care whether you are losing speed, but skidded turns will absorb your energy, and they lack the grace of a smooth cutting slice through the snow surface. Skidded turns are useful in the trees and bumps, but the carve is the way to go when in the pipe, when you want to go fast, and for general all mountain riding.

There are a number of key things to remember when working on carving. First of all, the steeper the edge angle of your board, the more the board will tip. Therefore, it is imperative to have a quiet upper body and flex the knees and ankles for balance. Your weight shift at the start is forward, about even in the middle, and weight should be back at the conclusion over the tail of the board. This is the only way to force the tail edge to go to the same place where the front has gone. Shoulders are parallel to the slope. A heelside carve should end looking as if you are sitting in a chair; the toeside carve has knees pressed toward the snow and chest and lower abdomen pushing outward. John Hobbs, Director of Snowboarding at Killington, calls that toeside body position "Full Turkey Dinner." The perfect carve soon becomes every snowboarder's goal.

Bumps

This book is supposed to be a basic introduction to snowboarding, not really a manual for advanced riders. However, once you are off the learning area, you will start to encounter bumped up snow surfaces. I once had an outraged student complain that the mountain should be ashamed of its grooming crew because the trail was not smooth. This was a person who had never before skied or snowboarded. He did not understand that bumps (moguls) are the result of skier/snowboarder turns where the snow gets pushed aside to the extent that it forms huge lumps which skiers have traditionally described in comparison to the size of Volkswagens.

There is a basic approach to riding bumps. First of all, you should have the proper attitude. If you look at the trail ahead as if you were in a pockmarked minefield and your life is in danger, you will not be very enthusiastic about your efforts to survive. Instead, tell yourself that the bumps are your friends. They are there to create a playground of fun. As to whether to go over or around, it sort of varies with the situation (icy or soft snow, close together or far apart bumps, *etc.*). Ideally, as a beginner at this, you should approach the bump, ride up to its crest, do a pivot turn, then do a straight slide down the back. This is the simplest method of attack, but it will only work in the simplest least sophisticated of bumps.

For a more advanced technique which often helps out in a mogul field, there is a free style move called a *shifty* similar to the skier's hockey stop in its powerful braking, allowing you to suddenly enact a change of direction. The board is slammed directionally across the hill as you pivot and slide down the back of the bump. Try to come up the side of the next bump and bounce off again with changed direction, continuing to move forward without stopping.

At a recent training clinic, AASI Examiner John Hobbs worked with a group of instructors exploring which were the best of varied techniques to apply when faced with a mogul field. Various maneuvers worked but some were more efficient than others; it was not a matter of using wrong techniques but more of seeking the most optimal of the choices. Upper body rotation can be employed to enact the necessary turn. Twisting the board (applying torque) can also be used to enact a similar turn. In addition, weighting the front into a strong pivot also works here. Hence, a variety of moves produce the desired result of turning the board, but to do the turn with the least effort and the most dexterity because of relying upon the engineered design of the board, your best choice is that of the pivot followed with the employment of torque. After that, you can then apply each and any other of the maneuvers. Be sure to keep directing the board down the fall line, keeping eyes looking ahead and weight forward. This is an example of the fact that there are many acceptable and even successful methods of attacking challenging terrain, but some ways will prove better than others.

Once you have been able to cross the first bump, ride over the next few in an up and down traverse, and then try to change direction with another pivot turn. Usually, turning on about every three or four bumps is a good way to begin to learn mastery as it offers you time to reassert your balance and your concentration. Stay focused and plan your strategy. The key ingredient in attacking a bump field is to keep your weight forward. You will quickly find that the very instant you tend to sit back, you will find yourself down and stuck cradled in the valley of the mogul.

If you have been a skier, do not rely upon past (skiing) knowledge of seeking a "zipper" line. This would be too tight a line for you to snowboard. As stated, start simple: just do several bumps then stop and look ahead. Remember the adage in the opening lesson that where you look is where you go. As you finish the turn you must direct your vision to where you plan to go next. Your body position should be low. Watch for bumps to practice on during the early season so that by the time spring comes around and the snow is soft, you will have developed the skills to handle those heavily moguled trails. The best circumstance is where the mogul field is partially groomed so that you can enter and exit dependant upon your commitment, expertise, and energy level.

Catwalks and Flats

I have a cat who seldom ever loses his balance, even when racing across the slick surface of uncarpeted floors or on narrow ledges. He not only has four legs but also a tail which all contribute to his agility. We, on snowboards, simply must learn to do our best with what we have: the board's sharp edges and our own quick reactions. Catwalks are trails which are too narrow to allow traverses or turns. They tend to be connecting paths joining the ski trails and therefore are usually well traveled. This means that they tend to be "skied off" in that the surface is slick from so much skier/snowboarder traffic.

On catwalks you won't always have room to do any turns, not only due to the narrowness of the trail but also because of the crowds of people. Therefore, the best thing is to travel on crossover trails with the 1-2-3 balanced turn rhythm but always going back to the initial edge. You will be holding your tilted edge then changing to flat then reverting back to the same edge again. Be sure that you stay on the uphill or inside section of the ski trail, hugging the upper area rather than heading to the lower trail edge with the danger of going off the side into the woods!

Your only actual difficulty in these situations is the cramping of your muscles from holding onto one riding edge for so long a time. That is why you have to give your aching legs a break by momentarily allowing the board to go flat.

Another tactic you can use to relieve aching muscles is to direct the board as far as possible riding up the uphill side of the trail, then doing a quick pivot turn back down onto the main highway and reverting back, changing edges again. A bonus of such a move is that not only does it help out tired leg muscles, but often there is an interesting stash of snow you can discover up on the side. This has the potential of transforming a boring trail into an interesting fun place.

Many times we ride an entire trail only to have difficulty at the very end where the runoff is flat. This is usually a situation where people simply underestimate the terrain challenge and tend to become distracted with the scene at the trail base. Here again is where the 1-2-3 rhythm is so essential in tilting the board:

1. original riding edge
2. go to flat with no edging
3. go to the opposite edge

Quickly repeat the process, but all done going straight ahead, not traversing. Practice makes perfect.

Remembering some of your earlier lesson pointers also helps out on catwalks and flats. You know that skidded turns slow you down, so use that as a means of speed control. Applying torsional flex to the board is also the way to go on catwalks. This bending of the board occurs when the front toes pressure upward while the back foot toes press down, thus creating a twisting of the snowboard. The heel edge is pressured at the nose of the board and the toe edge is engaged at the tail. The best way to understand the effect of torsional flex is to experience it by remembering to experiment often doing it.

Powder

You are in luck. The mountain has just received a gift from the heavens of over six inches of fresh powder. Western skiers have powder days all the time; eastern skiers treasure the occasions. For first lesson snowboarders, powder conditions are truly a blessing, mostly because they can't really do anything wrong. No matter how a person leans, the snow gently supports the board. That's why we instructors call it "ego snow." These are perfect conditions for learning: not too fast a surface and all movements are cushioned with errors forgiven.

The problem with having your first day snowboarding a powder day would be obvious tomorrow when the groomers would have packed down the snow. Then it will make a difference which edge of the board is tilted, and speed must be controlled. Second day snowboarders are always puzzled by their tremendous degree of success in the freshies just twenty-four hours ago, and now everything they do seems to be the wrong move. That was because the powder made all corrections for them; today the rider must do so himself.

For eastern riders, powder often causes a perceptual problem. We are so used to a hard pack surface that the vision of soft clumped snow causes our brains to react with warning. More familiar with frozen lumps affectionately called "death cookies," we simply are not accustomed to heaps of an undulating surface through which we can go straight on. The strategy I apply in these situations is to keep repeating to myself the words "whipped cream" to remind me that this is light and fluffy, and I can go into it without restraint.

The other way people have problems is because with a big dump of snow, you must allow the board to float. Your bindings may disappear from sight, and the board will sink deep into the snow which tends to make some riders react with anxiety. What you have to do is allow the board to float through the powder with your upper body rising and sinking, causing weighting and unweighting. Pressuring the board from tip to tail will cause it to "porpoise" which also means that you must ride it flat with only gentle tipping, no hard edging. The goal is that of flotation, but to float you need a degree of speed which will easily happen with that lack of edging and a flat board.

It is imperative to keep the nose (front end) of the board pointing upward, rather than allowing it to sink. To enhance this, some riders like to move their binding positions back slightly or even keep on hand another snowboard which is longer in length, specifically for use after a big dump.

Turns must be very round, never sharp, and knees must do the work as you first push against the snow and then retract your legs to pull up to board towards you which is the more difficult move. For specifics, you should have roughly 75% of your weight on the back foot and only 25% on the front. If you err and do the reverse, you will find yourself "over the handlebars." To initiate turns, 50%/50% works, but be sure to remember to shift back for the end of the turn resulting in a rising and sinking rhythmic motion of the board. Your mental image should be to go light as a bunny rabbit as you actually bounce your way down the trail. It's a heady feeling that's quite sweet.

A word of caution: do not get carried away by the excitement of all that powder and venture off the marked trail in violation of ski resort regulations and the Responsibility Code. Every season snowboarders die because they fall into tree wells and drown. Do not become one of those statistics.

Ice

Eastern riders all wish for powder days but we must learn to live with ice. Ice comes in different variations: blue ice, bullet proof ice, or those large frozen chunks called"death cookies." It's a fact of life that, even with the best grooming machines which crunch up the frozen surface into frozen granular, you will still risk encounters with ice. First of all, don't panic. Simply focus your eyes on the nearest place where there is snow cover and head for it. If you were driving your car and suddenly saw ice ahead, what would you do? Would you jam on the brakes? Certainly not! The same concept applies to snowboarding. Heavy edging will cause serious skidding and an out of control situation. Instead, have confidence that your snowboard has sharp edges (a good thing to have checked out at a tuning shop before setting out onto icy conditions), and allow that knife sharp edge to do its job. Think of the car braking image; cars steer into the path of a skid. Snowboarders should steer the tail edge of their board in the same path that the front edge has traveled. Recognize that move? You should be doing a carve.

Another reminder of how we cope with ice in everyday life is to think about how we navigate an icy sidewalk or parking lot. True, we tend to walk gingerly, but decisively. We are light on our feet, almost tiptoeing, and we look ahead to where it is safe to proceed. There is never a hard pushing on the heel or jamming down of the foot. Think of your board and its edges as a sharp knife slicing vertically downward rather than pushing horizontally across a surface. Follow these logical steps in terms of avoiding the horizontal skid by applying the cutting edge via the carve and moving decisively but cautiously to safety. Your goal is to get off the ice patch and head for snow, so focus your eyes on that destination. With an understanding of these moves, you should not ever allow yourself to be intimidated by the conditions. In fact, when you hear the loud scream of your board cutting into the icy surface it should actually give you a sense of empowerment.

Poor Visibility

You've purchased your lift ticket, you are ready to ride, but you can't see the mountain! This is really a personal call, but I suggest going into the lodge and making new friends. It is hard enough to find your way around with clear weather at a ski mountain. It's virtually impossible when blindfolded by fog. Even those who are familiar with the ski area will attest to the fact that fog is disorienting. You really can't tell uphill from downhill, and sound is so distorted that you don't know how close you are to other people on the trail.

Heavy snow is also similar to fog in that you will find yourself proceeding in a blind situation of a white-out. Experienced skiers and boarders know that sticking close to the edge of the trail along the tree line offers definition, but obviously, this also offers high risk of error and a danger of going off the trail into those trees! Conditions can vary within the ski resort itself. For example, at my home mountain of Killington we have six interconnected mountains. At any time one of them, Bear Mountain, will be in full sunshine while another, Killington Peak, has its own weather pattern and is totally obscured due to the weather conditions. Check trail maps and ask for guidance at the ski school or resort concierge desk. Just keep in mind my own personal motto: If you can't see it, don't ski it.

Trees

The first rule about tree riding is to never do it alone. At Killington we have signs posted which read "The mountains will be as cold tonight as they were 100 years ago. Don't ski alone." It's a terrible thing to be lost which happens easily in the woods, and it's even worse if you are alone. Being the object of a search parties might sound like a fun story to tell back at the ski lodge, but it's no joke to those doing the searching. Every season ski areas send out search teams for lost skiers or snowboarders who have gone under ropes to out of bound areas. You should be aware that at the end of the search, the lost persons are handed a serious bill to cover the costs involved. Helicopter search parties don't come cheap.

The second rule is to plan ahead. Remembering the visual joke of "plan ahea" with the "d" on the next line: you don't get up onto an elephant unless you know how to dismount; you don't enter the woods unless you have planned ahead where to exit. It is very easy to become disoriented in the woods and become totally lost. To satisfy the need, many resorts have areas specifically recommended for tree skiing and riding. Why do the trees? Why not? It's a challenge and the best snow is there: soft and deep. It just helps to go with someone who already knows the territory.

Before you enter, practice some riding skills such as riding tall and then short as you will have to crouch down to avoid branches. Hockey stops will be crucial. On the ski trail we can pick and choose where to turn; in the trees the terrain makes that determination. Before going in, try doing a follow-the-leader with your friend pursuing an irregular path. This will force you to abandon your regular turn rhythm and adapt to sudden unexpected movements. Because the tree areas are not groomed, you will encounter obstacles such as rocks and stumps which are not easily seen.

Beware of pushing at low hanging branches. I learned my lesson regarding this. While riding the trees adjacent to a trail, I reached out to push aside branches which meant that I had leaned forward to do so, weighting the front of my snowboard. This created a problem because I was in deep powder and, should have focused on keeping weight on the tail of the board. Well, down I went, with the nose of my board deeply buried and totally out of sight. I could not see my bindings and was caught in such deep snow that it was like quicksand. I reached down with one arm and it sunk into snow up to my armpit. My friend was ahead of me but hearing my calls, he exited the wooded area and started to walk back uphill on the trail in order to come to my aid. How did I get out? I realized that getting out of the binding would not accomplish anything, (the snow was too deep to stand in), so first I had to dig with my hands to remove the snow piled on the board which had so weighted me down. Then I rolled over crawling to a tree, reached out and dragged myself upright by hugging the tree and pulling my body weight upward. By the time my friend arrived, I had finally made it back standing, but it certainly wasn't easy. This is not an activity for the faint of heart, and obviously, not for beginner riders.

A much repeated warning: stay away from the bases of the trees. These are tree wells, and it is here that the soft snow piles high and deep. And it is here that snowboarders truly are in a quicksand situation. They sink down over their heads and actually drown. Be aware.

Oops...I almost forgot the third rule for tree riding. You know that where you look is where you go, so be absolutely sure to **look at the spaces, not the trees**!

Stance

In each of the above chapter sections there has been discussion of where to weight the board and the importance of knee and ankle flexion. The goal in snowboarding is to glide down the hill with flow and ease of movement. An athletic stance is crucial for such an accomplishment. Think of the body position taken in other sports. Football players are crouched ready to run, tennis players at net are ready for quick movements, knees bent, arms ready.

The important thing about a snowboarder's stance is that it is never fixed. You are constantly adjusting your balance as the terrain surface changes. In general, however, you should have slightly flexed knees and ankles. The stiff legged rider not only lacks good balance, he tends to bend at the waist and have his butt stick out. This is a means of compensating by lowering the center of mass. Little kids have a low center of mass and that's why they do so well when learning snowsports. Adults, particularly tall ones, wrongly try to lower their center of mass by crouching down on the board. It doesn't work in helping their balance. Instead, a flexed body position is not only more relaxed but helps absorb terrain irregularities.

I have discussed fore and aft but the main point is that this varies within the turn itself and due to snow conditions or terrain (*i.e.* powder or steeps). Weight on the front foot is the rule for learners, but as you progress, eventually the balance becomes 50% but such is only momentarily because you are moving and with motion comes the necessary changes.

Your hips should be slightly pointed forward in the direction of travel. The early years of snowboarding had riders facing front with hips across the board, but this twisted position is no longer necessary (or desirable) with the more modern board construction. Your body is sideways and thus your hips are subsequently angled.

Hands are a problem for some people. Beginners tend to wave their arms broadly "swimming" seeking aid in balance, but resulting in a subsequent drastic loss of balance. The upper body should be quiet. The front hand should be above the highback of the front foot. The back hand usually is above the thigh region of the back leg. Usually on turns this results in riding with one hand on either side of the board. For an emergency move in case of loss of balance, bring both hand up towards the nose of the board. This works to stabilize your position.

Eyes should be in the direction of travel. Look ahead. Know that with the peculiar sideways stance on a snowboard, one has a blind spot over your front shoulder. If you drive a car with a blind spot of road visibility, you learn to watch out for this liability. Do the same on your snowboard, especially because skiers are not aware of this problem and are not always able to anticipate the movements of a boarder. Same as on the highway: the right of way is something you can yield but do not have. As the rider ahead, you may have the right of way, but it's not so smart to suddenly turn and cut off an approaching person. It is also your responsibility to be aware of those around you, and it helps them to call out as you approach or overtake,"on your right" or "on your left."

Shoulders should be parallel to the slope. That might sound obvious, but it's not so easy to do when on steep terrain.

Your brain and body often insist upon leaning back into the hill. If you want to ride the slope on your board not on your butt, then you must lean forward down the trail. The steeper the hill, the more one shoulder should be tilted downward and the more forward you should be. As you make turns, the opposite shoulder should then be leading down. Remember those airplane turns? Do some of them and see that the downhill wing-arm should be lower than the uphill wing-arm. Happy flying.

QUESTION:

WHAT DO YOU CALL A SNOWBOARDER WHEN HE BREAKS UP WITH HIS GIRLFRIEND?

ANSWER:

HOMELESS.

CHAPTER 12
FREESTYLE MOVES, PARK, AND PIPE

One of the fun things about snowboarding rather than skiing is all the freestyle moves you can do. Snowboarding has evolved from skateboarding, so if you have done that sport then you will find that those actions you did on the pavement are rather easily adapted to doing on the snow. Of course, the obvious thing to do is sign up for a private lesson and have individual coaching. It would save many bruises. But, for those who prefer to check things out on their own, here are some guidelines.

Basic Spins

Up until now this book has stressed a quiet upper body with action initiated from the knees and ankles. That advice does not apply here. First, be sure to really review your switch riding. Only then will you be ready to try on-snow spins. These are fun to do and a distraction from working on skidded and carved turns. I once had a student who was totally frustrated, falling down each time he attempted a heelside turn. For a change of pace, I decided to try teaching him spins. It worked. After several on-snow 360's, only then did he relax enough and then was able to do a basic heelside turn.

Be sure that you are at a relatively flat place where it is quiet from traffic. Start to weight your front foot to initiate the heelside turn, looking in that direction. As the board comes around to its maximum point of travel uphill, now look in the opposite direction and weighting the back foot, ride switch. The board will turn and you will now be toeside. Weight the front foot now, look downhill, and you have done it.

Try the same thing in reverse, from doing a toeside turn to start, allowing it to spin as far as it will go uphill, rock back into switch, then complete the turn. If you are having difficulty picturing the task, consider the maximum distance of the initial turn to having the board pointing uphill, towards 12:00. As the board drifts back you steer it with weight change (riding switch) clockwise to 8:00 or 9:00. Then go forward to 6:00 and down the slope. That might clarify (or confuse) you further. People find one direction spin easier to do than the other. It varies with the individual.

Since you have done so well with the on-snow spin, how about trying to add a little air? A good starting point is to take off your snowboard and practice using your upper body to launch yourself into 180° spins and then trying 360° spins. For those who have forgotten their geometry, that means spinning halfway around and then completely around (A circle has 360 degrees). Your strength of wind-up plus looking in the direction of the spin are key. Of course, if you look down at the snow, nothing will work.

Getting back into your bindings, try doing a toeside turn pointing the board uphill. Now bend your knees and get ready to jump up, continuing in the direction you have been turning which is clockwise. Do what you did earlier without a board attached except that you won't need that wind-up because it will only add to the distance you must travel. As your legs extend, turn your upper body with arms held close.

Land with flexed knees to absorb the shock. This will take practice, but doesn't everything? The first times you attempt spins you will not be sure where your body is going. Then you will adjust. Just remember that when you skateboarded, it sometimes took all day to learn a simple trick. Be patient.

Ollies

If you ollied your skateboard, you will know how to do it on the snowboard. Basically, you spring up into the air using the stored energy in the tail of the board. Moving forward, bend your knees into a crouching down position, then shift weight to the board tail while forcefully yanking up the front of the board (by pulling up your front leg). Quickly extend; the board will soar up into the air. Be sure to land flat with weight evenly distributed on both legs.

Grabs

For some reason, I have never been interested in doing a grab. Maybe because I never thought it was particularly important (somewhat regional in popularity). Or maybe because I was never really great at bringing the board high up to my body. You need strong legs. But it does add style and pizzaz. As the board comes up to you, simply reach with your back trailing hand to hold an edge. Note that I said "simply," but it's not always so simple to do. If, instead of sucking the board up to your body, you reverse it, reaching down to the board and over to find the edge, then you will quickly lose balance and eat snow instead. Be sure to let go before landing.

Nose Rolls

The nose roll is the opposite of an ollie in that you instead press down the nose of the board while sucking up the tail. What makes it more interesting is that you rotate pivoting on the nose. This move really combines basic switch turns plus upper body rotation. It took me quite a while to learn the trick which was a requirement for my AASI Level II exam, and afterwards I was not so sure why it was important, except that it really is a fun thing to do (once you have mastered the technique). The front leg is extended as the back leg is yanked up hard; then, timed with a wind-up, you make a strong spinning movement of your upper body, turning your head into the direction of the spin. Either go 180° and ride off switch or do a total 360°. Review first by doing spins without the snowboard attached, then go back onto your snowboard and try sucking up the tail to lever on the nose. Last, try adding the spin. It's helpful to have a coach; I know this because a number of my fellow instructors had coached me, and it made a difference.

Jumps

First of all, start small. Using a mellow mound of snow, try your first jumps by approaching with bent knees, then standing up which adds to the dynamics as you spring off and are launched into the air. While airborne, again bend your knees bringing the board up toward your body and then extend to land. Some say that the take-off is the most important part, but I believe that the landing is more so. That is why you should first check out where you will land before attempting a jump, particularly if it is steep.

When at High Cascade Snowboard Camp in Oregon we did some serious jumps into wonderful deep powder. One of my friends failed to land with the board flat but instead the nose went straight down. His snowboard went deeply vertical, sort of like a candle on a birthday cake, leaving him hanging there not quite horizontally, held on by his bindings. It looked pretty funny, and he was lucky not to have broken both ankles. From then on none of our group ever forgot the importance of landing flat with weight evenly balanced between both feet.

Park

Before you even think about going into the park or pipe you should know that you will be entering a separate zone. There are specific unspoken (although often posted) rules here, and they are understood without anyone telling you. Watch how it works. Everyone waits patiently for their turn; there is no "cutting the line" even though people are spread out, and they are not actually lined up. Riders know who is first, and also some prefer to wait until they feel ready rather than to follow a sequence of order.

Once in the zoned off area, be quick about your business. Others are waiting, and they cannot safely begin their route until you are out of the way. When on the course you must remember that they usually cannot see you from their vantage point because of the built up structures, so you should be sure to get out of the way in case someone is already coming. Although there is no problem in the fact that the area is used by both skiers and boarders, the skier may not be aware of the snowboarder's blind side, another reason to be out of the way quickly.

These parks are special areas where you will want to try out those jumps you've been practicing on the trail, but know that here it is big time. There are table tops, rails and rainbows, and other constructions which all require a specific sense of timing and ability to balance with success. Park designs vary per individual resort, sometimes with specific parks for differing levels of riders.

Do not be intimidated by the table top, as long as you have done a lot of practice doing smaller jumps. Your approach requires a flat board. Many riders become spooked out because they can't see past the top and suddenly edge, thus scrubbing their speed and also their chance of success. Because there is often a steep landing, it's a good idea to first check out the jump by riding gently over it and then you will also understand the landing area.

Practice doing rails or rainbows before entering the park by trying to ride horizontally across a straight line which goes down the fall line. Use the ski tracks you see in the snow or look for the shadow under the chair lift cable. See if you can stay on top of the line. Then, when you are on a rail, the only difference is that of balancing perfectly centered on the board while moving downhill horizontally. "Only"? Easier said than done, but it certainly helps to know where your board centers. And the usual admonition: look ahead to where you want to go, not down at the rail.

Often there is a "spine" which simply looks like the back of a fish or dinosaur without the rising fins. Ride the spine and land at the end or instead bail out along the way via the sides. Quarterpipes offer practice for the big time challenge of the halfpipe. You can ride up the curved wall and experiment. Anything goes.

Pipe

When it is your turn to enter the pipe, if you are ready to go for it, you wave your hand, or yell out ("I'm dropping" or "I'm in"), being sure that everyone sees or hears you. Once in the pipe, you do your best, but do not tarry. You exit at the bottom, not climbing up the sides. And to hike the pipe, you do this outside the pipe, walking up the path on either side, never going up the pipe itself.

If this is your very first time, just entering is enough of a challenge. Always starting at the very top, ride up to the edge and then go straight in, across the pipe. This is really the same as entering a steep trail: point the board down over the edge, dropping your downhill (front) shoulder), front knee ready to extend. Say that you ride regular and have entered from the left. This means that you will be doing a toeside run up to the opposite wall. Do not try anything exotic. Instead, simply do a falling leaf, riding switch across the flat *(transition)* up the opposite wall. As you work your way down you can try a shallow turn (careful not to lose your momentum) and then do the rest of the run heelside. Go up one side (getting a *hit*), then ride switch for the next.

You will see that conditions may vary in terms of ice and steepness of the walls. If you do this exercise several times you will not feel so intimidated and also get a feel for the peculiarities of the surface conditions you are riding. One consolation is that the lower level rider you are, the safer you will be. You are not in any danger of zipping way up the sides and crashing doing a trick when changing edges. Also, for your level of riding, there is no danger of falling out over the sides.

With practice comes confidence. You should spend time outside the pipe working on short radius turns, carving, riding switch, and doing 180° hop turns. Do skidded turns. Use the entire trail in your turn; then use half the trail, then restrict your movements to one fourth of the slope. On steeper terrain, try turning uphill. Then go back into the pipe and try some turns at the highest point you can make it on the wall. My own coach years ago at Mt. Bachelor, Oregon, was Christine Sperber. She had advised me to think about going back down in the same place where I went up the pipe. This is good advice particularly because you will quickly learn how tiring it is to hike the pipe, so the more hits you get per run, the better off you are.

Just spend some time chilling out and watching what everyone else is doing. You will observe that similar to the way kids pump their legs to go higher when on a swing, you *pump* to enhance energy in the pipe. The trick is to start low, then swing arms upward as you go up the sides; the difficult part is that if you are too low or arms too loose, you will not have the right formula because you are moving on a slippery surface which will quickly throw you down.

The best way to avoid injury in the pipe is to take a private lesson. Also, you should absolutely not consider pipe riding without a helmet. One serious slam is a quick invitation to a concussion because the surface here is slick without the depth of powder you are accustomed to finding on the ski slopes. Body padding really helps, particularly wrist guards and tailbone pads. For those who fall easily on trail, perhaps the pipe is not your best option.

I'm not sure if AASI still uses this imagery, but years ago they used to liken snowboarding riding skill development to the structure of a martini glass. Look at the base of the glass, and see it as the core moves of the skidded turn which require mastery for basic snowboarding. Then, moving upward, the silhouette of the glass goes to the left and simultaneously to the right. These represent the two opposite destination poles of activity: one side for racers headed for the course and the other for freestylers enroute to the halfpipe. Freestylers do basic switch riding, then spins whereas in the other direction is basic carving. As to all that area in between, the center area holding the drink. This is the realm of all-mountain riding which includes mastery of steeps and bumps. The metaphor is apt in that most riders are in that large middle range: snowboarding on marked trails, out there making turns. No matter which is your style, they are all equally legitimate in terms of our definition of the sport. Snowboarding is about individuality and freedom of expression, and there is certainly plenty of latitude as to its defining action.

Ye olde
Snowboard Shop
SALE
Chickie.R

CHAPTER 13
YOU'RE COMMITTED

By now we should have reached your goal. The purpose was to get you to out there without major damage, to have you enter the world of snowsports, and to offer you the experience of snowboarding, assured of the fact that you will get hooked. It wasn't easy, certainly not the first day, but you have passed the trials of initiation. You have mastered the basic moves, have control of your board, and even might have ventured into the half pipe or the park. Of course, you are now stoked about boarding!

An unexpected bonus is to have known the serenity of the mountain landscape and experienced the beauty of nature first hand along with having a newfound respect for the mountain environment and understanding of winter's challenges. You are out there having loads of fun with your friends plus meeting new people. In essence, becoming a snowboarder has opened up a new world for you in which you now will be checking weather forecasts, clipping out articles on ski/snowboard resorts, watching for airline discounts, and spending your summer months waiting for winter.

Purchasing Equipment

At this stage, it would be advisable to go back and re-read Chapter 6, "The Three B's: Boards, Boots and Bindings," which was a prelude to getting involved in the more complex discussion which follows here. We look for specific elements when renting, but making a purchase certainly requires deeper analysis. In fact, if you are afraid that your patience will be exhausted with the variety of choices to be herein presented in equipment selection, be patient.

Did you ever read Herman Melville's *Moby Dick?* Aside from the plot of a megalomaniac sea captain in pursuit of the white whale called Moby Dick, there is one chapter devoted to whale classification, another on parts of the whale, then discussion of whales as they appear in art, another section on habits of whales, a discourse on whiteness itself...you get the general idea. Obviously, this book is not attempting to emulate a literary classic, yet Melville's book sets an example of explicitness in the understanding of a subject. I repeat; be patient in your reading of this chapter. Do not skip it. You will benefit from the advantage of knowing your extensive range of options before you are in the distracting environment of a retail shop.

Boots

The first piece of equipment for you to consider buying should be boots. We are all different, and these differences can be crucial in selecting the proper fitting boot. You can read all the advertisements, notice the brands which other snowboarders are wearing, and ask the salespeople at snowboard shops, but the bottom line is that the boot simply has to be the right fitting boot for you. Name brands are recommended based on their reputations, and a knowledgeable snowboard salesperson will guide you to the best purchase in terms of comfort, warmth and dryness. Remember that the money saved on a "special" will be of little consolation when you are out there with cold feet from damp boots or feel the chaffing effect of a poor fit.

What is a good fit? You should be trying on boots with the specific socks which you will be wearing when riding. If not, you would be wise to purchase snowboarding socks now before proceeding further. Buy several pairs because you will need them to wear with the boots on trips lasting more than one day(in case you were planning to do nightly handwash, forget it, because socks never dry in time). The boot should be snug and comfortable. Your heel should be firmly in place without gross slippage upwards. Walk around the store (hopefully you will have allowed quite a bit of time for this shopping project), leaning forward and backward, from toe to heel, then try rolling your toes from big toe to little toe. If the boot is truly comfortable, you will be assured of having proper blood circulation, and your feet will be warm.

I recently purchased a boot which was a proper fit, but turned out not to be warm enough. My local Killington resource was at Peak Performance, a ski shop, where board certified pedorthist David Strousse offered me a creative solution. He switched the liner (the removable inner "bladder" part of the boot, separate from the outer shell) of my snowboard boot and substituted it with a really warm liner from a ski boot. The result is my own unique hybrid of a ski boot liner matched with the step-in snowboard boot necessary for coordination with my binding system. It works.

A good boot fitter can do a lot. There are heel or ankle lifts and padding of all sorts. As stated in my own case, liners can be adjusted or even exchanged, and pressure spots can be eliminated. That, in itself, is the most important reason to shop where skilled boot fitters are on the job. It's like selecting a good medical specialist. Choose a person who does his specialty exclusively, not someone with a general practice

The best boot fitters are found at the most popular ski areas where they therefore have the most experience in fitting problems or are located at a quality (usually large city) ski shop. Look for the America's Best Bootfitters emblem on display, or go to their Web site at www.bootfitters.com for a listing of shops which employ certified boot fitters.

Another source of recommendation is the ski school. Ask your instructor where to go for boots. Also, as in my personal experience, do not limit yourself to only patronizing snowboard shops for boot fitting adjustments. Experienced ski shop bootfitters have been around for a very long time, and boots are boots, no matter how they function.

Some of us have feet which turn inward, others turn outward, arch heights vary, *etc*. To address such issues, a really good thing to have are custom footbeds, even if you do not have glaring boot fit problems. The footbed assures proper alignment which will create better balance when out on the hill. These are not the expensive medical orthotics you might have in mind. They are custom molded innersoles and are not overly costly or particularly complicated to have made. Ski/snowboard shops have special machines which create footbeds when you stand on innersole molds. These become shaped in response to heat application. It doesn't take long to create the impression, and once you have them made, they will last through the lifetimes of several pairs of boots.

Remember that, as the saying goes, your ride depends on "where the tire hits the road." Your boot fit is crucial to proper snowboard movement and balance because the boot provides the first link between the body movement of your foot via the binding to the board itself. The best on snow performance is predicated upon response from your feet, so skillful riding really starts back in the sales section of the snowboard shop when you select your boots.

Another aspect to be considered is what kind of riding you plan on doing while wearing them. Some boots are soft as slippers while others as stiff as those ski boots you were happy to put aside. Ability to flex is what you want to check out, and large footed persons should give preference to a less bulky boot which will avoid the problem of toe or heel drag. Style? The main influence on boot style is not that of high fashion design, but rather streetwear as seen in skateboarding styles. Basically, we've all come a long way since the early years of snowboarding when footgear was pretty much limited to Sorels.

Now that you are purchasing boots, it is a good idea to buy some sort of a boot dryer. Feet perspire, and the insides of your boots will be quite damp by the end of the day. Unless you take serious measures to remedy the wet boot situation, you will be a very unhappy person tomorrow morning if you must start the day with cold damp boots. There are numerous boot dryer products on the market, and your best place to seek them out is at a ski area where you can shop around.

For a number of years I have been using a system made by Evaporator which blows cool air. It has a total of four outlets with varied size nozzles to dry either two sets of boots or one set of boots and a pair of gloves. The unit even comes in a case which is perfect for travel. Another less expensive system I have found handy is Happy Feet, a set of rods which conduct heat. Minimal in design, they do the job. Using a hair dryer is always available as a last resort, but purchasing a boot dryer is certainly the wiser way to go.

Board

Selecting a snowboard can definitely be a mystifying and overwhelming proposition. There are so many companies who make snowboards that it's really a daunting project. A starting place would be to check out what the pros recommend. Snowboarding magazines such as *Transworld Snowboarding, Snowboarder Magazine*, or *Snowboard Life* usually devote their fall issues to an annual buyer's guide. Since there's no way you can personally test ride all those boards, find out what the experts liked and why. It's the business of professionals to know what is really good. Take their advice as opposed to that of a shop eager to unload its inventory. That's a starting point, then relate their picks to your personal needs. The next step is to study different company catalogs. Then, being honest in your self evaluation of riding ability, try to arrange a demo, and make your best judgement call. Good luck.

If you have looked at the board racks of a snowboard shop or studied any company brochures, you will be aware that there are many choices offered in snowboard design, and this does not refer merely to the graphics. You will need a good sales person as your guide, and you must honestly state your level of experience and expertise. Dependent upon a rider's ability skills, snowboards range from entry level beginner boards to those for advanced or expert riders. Next, discuss whether you will be doing freestyle or all mountain riding. Then focus on the factors of length, width, and *flex*. Handling and performance are influenced by internal composition, *flex* (how easily the board bends or twists), board shape, and basic construction.

First of all, you will eliminate certain boards simply by using the criteria of how experienced you are. Next you should focus on what type of riding you choose to do: whether you want to race, do freestyle in the half pipe and tricks in a snowboard park, or prefer what is called freeride which is all mountain riding. If you are going to concentrate on racing, then you will want to make your selection based on a number of racing boards available (remember that these must go with a hard boot and clamp binding set up). All mountain riding, versus freestyle, offers a wide range of selection and many boards are suitable for crossover activity. All mountain means what it says: good all over the mountain whether it's on trail or in the trees, on bumps or groomed terrain. Freestyle boards tend to be shorter with a different stance hole pattern more towards the center, and are softer for ollieing, although halfpipe riders prefer a stiffer tail.

The next thing to consider is length. Boards are measured in centimeters which is hard for Americans who have never succumbed to mastering the metric system. Therefore, the seemingly slight variation of the board measurements tend not to have a lot of meaning for us, a dangerous wrong assumption. In general, when set up standing in front of you, the board should come somewhere in the area zone near your nose. Not too scientific.

Desirable length also varies in terms of where you plan to ride. For example, if you are headed for the park, your freestyle board should be closer to shoulder height because shorter boards are quicker to turn. On the other hand, if you are going freeriding (general all mountain riding), you will want something a bit longer, nose height, when the board is standing on its tail. For those who enjoy speed, length adds stability when going very fast. An additional factor to consider in selecting length is whether you will be doing a lot of powder riding which definitely does better with a longer board.

Some boards are designed to ride forward only, whereas others go easily in both directions, forward and back. This is referred to as *directionality.* The all mountain boards can work okay doing park and pipe, but were designed for those who usually spend most of their riding time down mountain trails whether a mogul field, steeps, or groomed terrain They are engineered to go smoothly mostly in one direction but can offer the versatility of still being able to ride switch.

For the freestyler, on the other hand, in terms of board orientation, there should be no difference which direction you are headed on the snowboard. That is why the twin tip boards were developed. Frontwards is also backwards. It's easy to understand the value of those twin tip boards if you are doing spins and tricks, hanging out in the park They have duplicate head /tail shaping thus have the option of riding easily in either direction. The *nose* (front) is the same shape as the *tail* (back). In such a situation you would then also want a board with some snap so that you can pop off the tail doing ollies. You will certainly want a quick responding board for sudden moves and a solid platform for landings after jumps, if all that is in your plans for the future. Pipe riders tend to select a board with stiffer tail as holding an edge and snappy responsiveness are among their main criteria.

The very best way to make a judgement is to "demo" a board. These are the sample boards available for demonstration (rental cost is usually applied to purchase price). The problem will be that of available inventory in finding one of the correct length for your body weight and riding ability. In any event, you can still get an idea of how the board reacts, even if it is not a perfect fit.

Snowboard shop salespeople tend to use language that doesn't have much meaning for you. For example, they talk about a stiff board as opposed to a "noodle," and how some boards are "more forgiving." Knowing what is involved in the design elements of a snowboard will help. Otherwise, these are just words. The vocabulary list in Chapter 3 gave some definitions, but hang in there, because here comes more technical information to better prepare you in terms of understanding it all.

Length has been mentioned, but there are other measurements. The waist width (size at the narrowest part where bindings are placed) is always given. This is crucial for people with larger boot sizes as too narrow a waist will result in toe or heel drag. Also definitely less desirable for beginners, a board with a very narrow waist will require the extreme angles of a very aggressive stance for the binding (usually these are the racing boards). Although the wider waist board lacks the quickness of turning power, in compensation it will offer additional stability and give an easier ride. Too narrow is an obvious problem, but too wide is also in the negative zone. If the board is too wide then one cannot directly pressure the edges which means that you will have a great deal of difficulty initiating a turn. It's a Goldilocks and the 3 Bears situation: choose the waist width that fits not too narrow, not too wide, but just right.

Then, there are the double elements of *sidecut* and *effective edge.* Think of turn shape on the snow as an outline from the edge of a circle. The sidecut radius is in direct proportion to the radius of that circle. Another way to explain it is that the silhouetted shape of the board, the effective edge, is the edge area that actually touches the snow. That is what influences the actual shape of your turns, a result of the sidecut. If you make short radius turns (advanced riders), you want a board with smaller sidecut radius resulting in a decreased sidecut which enacts a sharper turn. This may not be so noticeable to your untutored eye, but the sidecut is dramatically illustrated when looking at the extremely pronounced shape of the racing board, enabling it to fly past the gates with sharp turns. Those who prefer larger longer turns will go for the increased sidecut. In essence, the larger the radius, the larger the circle, and the more mellow the turns.

Effective edge is really the more realistic measure of board length as it refers to how much of the metal edge of the board actually comes in contact with the snow. You can feel the difference when riding boards of different effective edge as the more edge touching snow, the more controlled ride you will have. Of course, you don't really use all of that edge from nose to tail anyway. When making a turn, the very front tip area of the board will not come into play, but the concave arc of the side is what contacts the snow surface when pressure is applied to the board. In fact, when purchasing your board, be sure to have the shop "detune" the nose of the board some five to six inches down on each side so that it will not grab as you initiate a turn.

The shop salesperson may lean the board against a wall and push against it to show bendability. We call this *flex*. Boards must have enough flex to bend while you ride them without breaking, sort of like a shock absorber. A beginning snowboarder will find it difficult to make turns on a stiff board. Keep in mind your body weight as a factor, and that softer boards are more forgiving for less experienced and lighter weight riders. Softer flex allows those nice C shaped turns for general all mountain riding. Stiff boards are for hitting it hard at high speeds, but will you be going there at your level? Flex is enacted both from nose to tail of the board along its length, and also one speaks of torsional flex which is twisting, so crucial in making carved turns.

Unless having the experience of doing a demo, you will have to rely upon the snowboard company's written materials and the salesperson to judge the importance of these varied elements in your situation, all in conjunction with your riding ability. Usually, the more advanced the rider, the more he wants the board to do, hence the requirement for a stiffer board.

Always keep in mind that ability level, terrain selection, and body weight are the key factors. Your weight is a very important factor in this equation. Fortunately, there are charts (usually on a sticker attached to the board base) specifying weight range for the various sized boards

All people ride differently, and the perfect board for your friend will not necessarily suit you. I once purchased a board which came very highly recommended not only in trade magazines but also from another instructor. Unfortunately, as I mentioned is commonly the case, the demo available was not the length I needed (too long), so I had attributed my less than perfect ride to the need for a different size. I bought the board anyway, convinced by so many endorsements, just ordering it in a shorter length. My mistake was that the company's product guide range for weight was rather broad, and although my weight appeared on the chart, it was at the very minimum which was really a bit too light to sufficiently handle the stiff construction. I eventually adjusted, but it certainly took a conscious effort. Since then I have found the board which works the best for me and each season order the newest model.

Camber is a word you may hear which is the term used to describe the stored energy latent in a board. You may notice that when placed flat on the floor, the center section has a slight rise. Sometimes this is more easily visible with skis. When a ski or snowboard turns, it goes into reverse camber, and that rise now becomes a depression which acts as a pivot point pressuring downward. In essence, the more camber, the more lively and snappy is the board and the quicker responding. Too much camber can be hard to handle; slightly less camber can provide a more leisurely ride. After extensive usage, advanced age, or poor care, the camber will disappear, and a snowboard will lose its liveliness. The dead response to your riding movements will send a message that it is now time to shop for a replacement.

Snowboard catalogs will give you a full explanation of the uniqueness of their product's board construction. The real problem with making a board choice is because the various boards are actually much less similar than you might think. Since they do not have the same internal construction, they will ride quite differently, even if they are of equal length and alike in designation of purpose. Think of the board as a series of layers with filler between the base and top sheet. Internal materials may range from wood core to fiberglass layers, carbon fiber strips, kevlar, resin, types of foam or even bamboo.

It's not that one is better than all others; it's just that each construction results in different responsiveness, and you really must consider the importance of that which cannot be seen. This inner construction is what creates the snap and power of a board and allows it to give a signature ride. The choice of *sandwich* versus *cap* design refers to the sealing in of the material between the outermost layers. Cap construction wraps the entire package in fiberglass up to the metal edges, whereas sandwich stacks the interior layers and then covers the edges with a sidewall. All of these factors make a substantial difference which is why there are so many snowboard brand choices.

Notice that I have not specifically mentioned a single snowboard manufacturer or given any web sites. That is primarily because there so very many companies who are making so many styles of boards for so many different types of terrain with the additional variant of suitability for different conditions (*i.e.* powder vs. hardpack). Remember that the board your friend loves to ride is not necessarily the board you will enjoy. The board I like may be one you would hate!

You certainly don't pick a board based on its graphics, although upon occasion, I have had a student do so, sometimes with disastrous results. However, you really don't want to ride a board all day looking down on something really ugly, so one should not discount the influence of packaging. Luckily, at this time there is a wide variety of really creative art work to be seen out there. In fact, I often advise friends in art school that snowboard graphic design has great potential. It relates to graffiti plus street art plus fine art. Now that putting stickers on a board has become totally out of fashion, the graphic has necessarily become more identifiably important to the snowboard purchaser. It's often hard to resist the appeal of a great looking board.

Bindings

This is just a reminder that your bindings will be determined first of all by whether you are going the hard boot or soft boot route. Then, if a soft boot, it really becomes a matter of step-in versus buckle. Refer back to the discussion of this issue in Chapter 6, and remember that the most important factor is boot fit. You may want to have a certain step-in, but the boot must be compatible with the binding, and if the boot is not comfortable, then you really cannot consider that binding. That is the twinning problem of step-ins in that each binding system works only with that company's matched boot.

When they first appeared, step-in bindings were hailed as the way to go. No more crouching down to buckle, a particular boon for those who hate deep knee bends, and you wouldn't have to sit down on the snow. Years have gone by and it's been a test of time in which for many riders the system's disadvantages seem to have outnumbered these advantages. The pluses are speed of entry and exit, but the negatives are the ice and snow which clump and freeze to the metal mechanism, and the fact that the step-in binding is less responsive in terms of performance. Note that company catalogs now offer a variety of buckle style bindings and only a few, if any, step-ins. This seems to be a sign for the future demise of the step-in binding. Personally, I use step-in bindings, mostly because of the fact that when instructing I am constantly stepping in and out of my bindings. My needs are not the same as yours.

Years ago there used to be heavy discussion as to high-backs versus lowbacks. When making a heelside turn, as you now know, you must go forward pressuring with the ankle. This move requires some sort of a support: hence, the piece which rises vertically from the back at the heel end of the binding. Initially, highback supports were designed about 8 inches high. Then came the impact of skateboarders upon snowboard engineering, and the result was a *lowback*, only half the size, which was more stylish looking and particularly popular with young riders. Highback vs. lowback became something of a hot issue with some preferring the less obtrusive device whereas others differed in opinion, even among freestylers, some of whom argued that the highback assists in getting air because it offers necessary support to the calf of the leg when going up the wall of the halfpipe.

That may not be far up there on your list of requirements, but the advantage of a highback, along with offering support on the heelside turn, is the *flad* (forward lean adjustment). If you play around with different positions you will become aware of its role in guiding you on those heelside turns. The higher the flad angle, the quicker the heelside response. There is also the additional element of adjustable highback rotation. It should be rotated parallel to the edge of the board for the most powerful direct response. Low backs seem to be out of style by now anyway.

If you do go for step-ins, you should be aware that the highbacks of step-in bindings can either be exposed (external) or they are incorporated into the boot which is required to match the set up. When trying on boots with internal highbacks, ask the sales person about the forward lean adjustments. There are two advantages of an external highback. One is that of ease in forward lean adjustment (flad) and the second, perhaps more important element, is that to have the stiff highback on the board rather than inside the boot which certainly makes for a great deal more comfort when walking in your snowboard boots. Leave that stiff backing on the board itself rather than rising up from the heel area inside your boot.

Buckle bindings offer more flexibility in that you select your boot based on comfort and fit and then decide which binding to purchase, mostly based on your bank account balance. Standing on a lift line and looking at people's equipment, you can easily see that there's been a lot of design change lately in bindings. Some have a toe strap which looks like the chinstrap of a helmet and easily recognizable are those of a company called Flow which has a fabric covering extending from what is usually the toe strap area to well above where the ankle strap would be. Those are some visible differences, but there are others which cannot be seen.

High-performance, heel-hold, and forgiving flex are the key by-words of the industry today. Adjustable heelhoops, nylon, carbon, polycarbonate, or aluminum baseplates, varied range of flexes, tool free flad adjustments, revised highback rotation systems, no need to scrape off boot sole snow, better padding, improved ratcheting—these are all the latest design features. Quality binding systems are crucial to your snowboarding as they form the key reaction link from your boot contained foot to the board. For this reason I tend to advise going for the best that you can afford. Price can be a way to help determine quality. Consider what you expect from the binding in relation to what type of snowboarding you plan on doing (*i.e.* halfpipe, freestyle, *etc.*). Before sealing the deal, be absolutely sure that your boot fits easily in and out of the binding plate and also that you understand completely the mechanisms involved.

Care of Your New Purchases

Ski areas offer season tunes or you can pay as you go, but for most people it is helpful (and financially prudent) to know something of caring for the equipment yourself. There are two areas of maintenance in regard to the snowboard: the edges and the base.

Edges should be sharp, especially as you want them to hold you on icy surfaces. It is not difficult to learn how to deburr those rough snags on the edges. Ask an experienced friend or shop tuner to demonstrate for you the use of a stone to deburr, but leave the board at a shop to have edges done when they are in need of sharpening. The problem with doing the edges yourself is that, unless you really know what you are doing, you can destroy the bevel. It's not like getting a lousy haircut which eventually grows out. Hair grows back, but snowboard edges that are filed off will have that metal gone forever.

Taking care of the base is another story. First of all, it helps to understand the role of wax. Movement of a board over the snow surface creates friction which results in heat, causing snow particles to melt into droplets of water upon the board base. Bad enough that the wetness slows you down, but then these drops refreeze and clump up during the time that they move along towards the tail of the board. Wax is what allows you to slide, since it reduces the friction and prevents water adhesion to the snowboard base.

Ski and snowboard racers are the gurus of waxing. Their success depends not only upon their skill in riding a course but also in selecting the wax which will help them go the fastest. For the rest of us, knowledge of the basic categories will suffice. You should have wax sticks of the basic color trio: yellow for warmest temperatures (32º), red for warm (27º), and green for cold (16º-0º).

Gather up the following items necessary to do a tuning:

1. an old sheet or tablecloth to use as a drop cloth because wax shavings will fall to the floor
2. the least expensive most basic iron you can find
3. a triangle shaped scraper
4. citrus cleaner, purchased at a ski/snowboard shop
5. some clean rags for use with the citrus cleaner
6. Scotch-Brite pads (sold at a supermarket in the section where they sell kitchen cleaning supplies and dishwashing soap)

Spread the drop cloth on the floor and get set to become a tuning-tech.

Step #1: Lay the board flat either on the floor (although certainly not the best positioning as then you must work on your knees) or preferably propped up between two chairs. Obviously, a pair of tuning bench "horses" would be the best choice. Using a triangle shaped scraper you will be able to pull off some of the old wax, going from tip to tail. Then clean the base following instructions on the citrus cleaner. This will remove any remaining old wax and dirt.

Step #2: Heat the iron at most on medium setting, and, holding the wax stick perpendicular to it, allow dribbles of wax to drop down onto the board. Generously create a modern art style abstract pattern of wax polka dots over the entire base surface. Watch out for your fingers as the wax stick burns down very quickly.

Step #3: With a low to medium setting (you don't want to scorch the surface), lightly iron the board. **You must keep the iron moving** as you gloss over those drops of wax, spreading them onto a smooth surface across the base, trying not to coat the metal edges.

Step #4: Allow the wax to cool and harden. This will take at least 20-30 minutes, or preferably let it sit overnight.

Step #5: You did such a nice job ironing on all that wax. Now it is necessary to scrape it off. Using that triangle shaped scraper, pull towards you, working vertically from tip to the tail area.

Step #6: Using either a Scotch-Brite pad or even a scouring sponge (no soap), polish the base. Again, movement should not be circular but vertical, from tip to tail.

It's a good idea to gather together these tuning items and assemble a kit. You will appreciate its existence if you happen to go away on a trip and experience sudden extreme temperature changes. A board with the wrong wax will simply not glide. It barely moves at all. Another option is to pack a tin of snowboard wax along with an application sponge and wiping cloth. That will give you a quick fix without getting involved in a waxing project. Either way, check out the necessary materials needed for waxing before the crisis situation arises.

On the other hand, even if you are really good at doing the wax routine, you should occasionally take the board to a shop for a professionally done job. Gouges and deep scrapes from rocks or debris ridden trails require sophisticated treatment and know-how for proper repair. You will learn to appreciate the importance of a good waxing to insure a smooth ride along with the tuned board's sharpened edges for firm holding on icy slopes.

Off Season Storage

Heat rises. Therefore an attic is the warmest part of a house and not a happy place for winter sport equipment. Instead, select a cool dry area for off season storage. One of my friends stores his snowboard on the floor under his bed. Boots also should be in a moderate temperature area. Clean your boots, dry them inside and out, stuff with paper towel (this keeps out spiders), lace, and buckle them up. If you are really a neatie, you may want to store your boots in a container to keep them free of what will be a six month layer of surface dust.

Check the binding for loose or missing screws. The board will require a bit more attention. Remember the wax instructions? Follow steps 1-4. What you want now is an extra heavy coat of protective wax which will sit on the board until you scrape it off a half year later. If you haven't mastered the ironing technique or haven't had the board tuned during the season, this would be a good time to drop it off at a shop, have the edges done, the base checked out, and let them give it that heavy wax coating. Either way, with this minimal end of season care, you will be ready to go with the earliest flurries of next winter.

Wash your outerwear jacket and snowboard pants, remembering that even though powder leaves a residue, it is preferable over liquid soap which takes away water repellence. Just for good measure, be sure to spray with Scotch-Guard. An excellent product I have used is Red Wash. To quote the bottle, "No, dummy, it doesn't turn your clothes red." By its attitude, one tends to assume it is a snowboard product. Distribution may be local only, as the label origin only states Red Corp, Burlington, VT. At any rate, it is effective for cleaning down filled and synthetic insulated garments. Another product you can look for is Revivex, developed by the makers of Gore-tex fabric. "Specifically engineered for Gore-tex, Activent, and Dryloft products," this spray will restore water repellent finishes. Go to them on the Web at www.gorefabrics.com for dealer listings in your region.

That's it! You have learned about snowboarding from start to finish, from first purchases to final details. Now that the season is over, be sure that you use the time off constructively. Let's be honest with ourselves, and instead of just focusing on what a great time you had snowboarding, remember how stiff you were after the first day out on the hill. The calves of your legs ached, and your body was weary. You had muscle pain from muscles you didn't know existed!

Here is your chance. Use the off season months to really get into shape. Join a health club, have a regimen of walking, start running, try biking, try wind surfing, revive your old skateboard. Read about the benefits to doing weights, and buy yourself a set of dumbbells. What is really being implied here is that because of your snowboarding, you have become committed to a different lifestyle. You may never have thought of yourself as athletic or an outdoors person. Perhaps you were even someone who never cared for winter weather Unexpectedly, you now regard the summer months as a period of readiness for what has suddenly become your preferred season of winter. You should be motivated to indulge yoursel in a newly revised self image, all because you have attained your goal of learning to snowboard.

Congratulations, rad dude, you rule!

F.A.Q.

FREQUENTLY ASKED QUESTIONS

Question: Why does my board shoot forward out of control?

Answer: You have too much weight concentrated toward the tail of the board, most probably because your upper body is leaning backward. This is a natural reaction of your brain telling your body that you must be crazy to lean forward while heading downhill. Try to maintain a more centered stance and stay on less steep terrain.

Question: Why do I keep falling when trying to turn onto my heelside?

Answer: You must allow the board to go flat between the sequence of toeside onto heelside. The problem usually arises because your vision looks downhill during that period of edge change. Focus your eyes across, not down the hill, and be sure that you allow the turn to be rounded in shape. Heelside does not mean leaning back onto your heels; see page 101.

Question: What caused me to crash forward onto the snow doing a face plant?

Answer: You mistakenly put your weight on the downhill edge of your snowboard.

Question: Why does my board "chatter" on a steep slope?

Answer: You are putting too much pressure on the board because you are instinctively leaning back into the hill.

Question: Why do I seem unable to look ahead and instead keep looking down ?

Answer: Looking at the board is usually a reaction to

nervousness and lack of confidence. Stay on easy terrain until you have better control which will enable you to look up and ahead.

Question: After riding awhile, I get a nagging pain in my back leg. Is this because of my binding setting?

Answer: Your binding is set too close to zero which creates undue pressure when you bend your knees. Dial it up a bit to a higher number and see if your knee can bend more easily. Also, check if your legs are too far apart. The distance between the centers of each binding should be close to your shoulder width; see page 84.

Question: How can I go faster without being out of control?

Answer: Heading more into the fall line will increase your acceleration, but the key for speeding up is to make carved, not skidded, turns.

Question: I've seen photos of myself snowboarding and I do not look cool. Either my butt sticks out or I look like a standing stiff. What is the better stance?

Answer: A good stance is one that is constantly changing, but, in general, you should stand with knees supple, ready to absorb the irregularities of the terrain. As to your butt, that is because you are bending over at the waist instead of bending at your knees. This is particularly a problem with tall people who try to stabilize themselves on the board by lowering their center of mass.

Question: I have been riding for a while but don't seem to get better. Any suggestions?

Answer: Stay on easier not harder terrain, and take a lesson.

Question: How does snowboarding change your life?

Answer: You become part of a great outdoor fraternity!

INDEX

PERSONAL NOTES

THESE PAGES ARE FOR YOU TO KEEP TRACK OF YOUR OWN SNOWBOARDING HISTORY. WRITE DOWN THE DATE, RESORT, INSTRUCTOR'S NAME, AND WHAT YOU HAVE LEARNED. YOU WILL BE AMAZED AT THE RECORD OF YOUR PROGRESS! IT'S ALSO A HANDY PLACE TO WRITE THE NAMES AND ADDRESSES OF THE NIFTY PEOPLE YOU HAVE MET.

PERSONAL NOTES